ESSENTIAL GUIDE TO
CAPITAL MARKETS

Publisher: One11 Publishing, LLC
Printed in the United States of America
First Edition: June 2023
ISBN Paperback: 978-1-7343537-5-4

By Selamawit Teshome

@SelamTeshomeHM

June 2023

TABLE OF CONTENTS

PREFACE

Welcome to the world of Capital Markets!

First things first, what are capital markets? Simply put, they are platforms where companies and governments can raise funds by selling securities to investors. These securities can be stocks, bonds, or other financial instruments.

Now, you might be thinking, "Why should I care about capital markets?" Well, for starters, they play a crucial role in driving the global economy. The flow of capital through these markets helps to fuel economic growth and development.

But beyond that, capital markets can provide opportunities for individuals to grow their wealth. By investing in securities, you can potentially earn returns that outpace inflation and increase your net worth over time.

Of course, investing in capital markets is not without risk. The value of securities can fluctuate based on a variety of factors, such as economic conditions, company performance, and global events. That's why it's important to educate yourself on the ins and outs of this world before diving in.

That's where this guide comes in. Throughout the upcoming chapters, we'll delve into everything from the fundamentals of stocks and bonds to derivatives and collective investment schemes. We'll also examine the mechanisms of capital markets, taking a closer look at the roles played by regulatory entities, service providers, and other capital market participants. Finally, we'll explore major stock exchanges worldwide and gain an understanding of how significant capital market crashes have shaped the industry.

So whether you're a seasoned investor or a curious newcomer, we hope that this guide will serve as a valuable resource as you explore the exciting world of capital markets. Happy reading!

CHAPTER I

WHAT ARE CAPITAL MARKETS?

Capital markets are financial markets in which long-term debt (over a year) or equity-backed securities are bought and sold, in contrast to a money market where short-term debt is bought and sold. Capital markets are the lifeblood of a thriving economy. They provide the necessary channel for the flow of funds from those with surplus savings to those who are in need of capital.

A capital market can be either a primary market or a secondary market. In a primary market, new stock or bond issues are sold to investors, often via a mechanism known as underwriting. The main entities seeking to raise long-term funds on primary capital markets are governments (which may be local or national) and business enterprises (companies). Governments issue only bonds, whereas companies often issue both equity and bonds.

In a secondary market, existing securities are bought and sold between investors. The secondary market is much larger than the primary market, and it is where most of the trading in capital markets takes place. The secondary market provides liquidity for investors, which means that they can easily buy and sell their securities without having to worry about finding a buyer or seller. It also provides price discovery, which means that investors can see what other investors are willing to pay for a particular security.

There are a number of different types of securities that can be traded in capital markets. The most common types of securities are stocks, bonds, and derivatives. Stocks represent ownership in a company, and they give investors a share of the company's profits. Bonds are loans that are issued by governments or companies, and they pay investors a fixed interest rate. Derivatives are financial instruments that derive their value from other assets, such as stocks or bonds.

Capital markets are a complex and ever-changing system. However, they play an essential role in the economy, and they provide a number of benefits to businesses, investors, and the economy as a whole.

One of the primary benefits of capital markets is that they provide a crucial source of financing for companies. Businesses can issue stocks or bonds to raise funds, which can then be used to invest in new projects, expand operations, or pay off existing debts. This access to capital allows businesses to innovate and grow, which in turn creates jobs and drives economic growth.

Capital markets also provide a way for governments to fund their operations. Governments can issue bonds, which are bought by investors, to finance projects such as infrastructure development, education, and healthcare. These investments can have a significant impact on the economy, creating jobs and improving the lives of citizens.

Furthermore, capital markets allow investors to diversify their portfolios. By investing in stocks and bonds, investors can spread their risks across different companies and industries, reducing their exposure to any one company or sector. This diversification can help investors weather market fluctuations and protect their investments.

In addition to these benefits, capital markets also play a crucial role in promoting transparency and accountability. Companies that issue securities are required to disclose information about their operations, finances, and risks. This information allows investors to make informed decisions and hold companies accountable for their actions.

Despite all these benefits, there are also risks associated with capital markets. One of the most significant risks is the potential for market volatility. Stock prices can fluctuate rapidly, leading to significant losses for investors. Additionally, economic downturns can lead to a decrease in demand for financial instruments, making it more difficult for businesses to secure funding.

Another risk is the potential for fraud and misconduct. In an effort to raise capital, some companies may engage in unethical or illegal behaviour, such as misrepresenting their financial statements or misleading investors. These actions can ultimately harm the economy by eroding investor confidence and reducing the amount of capital available for legitimate businesses.

Finally, there is also the risk of systemic issues. Capital markets are interconnected, and a failure in one area can have far-reaching effects. For example, the 2008 financial crisis was caused by a combination of factors, including a housing market bubble and the widespread use of complex financial instruments. The resulting collapse of the housing market had ripple effects throughout the economy, ultimately leading to a global recession.

Conclusion

Capital markets play a vital role in any economy, providing businesses and individuals with access to funding and investment opportunities. However, like any financial system, capital markets come with risks. It is important for investors and regulators to be aware of these risks and take steps to mitigate them. When managed properly, capital markets can be a powerful force for economic growth and prosperity.

CHAPTER II

THE ROLE AND RESPONSIBILITIES OF A CAPITAL MARKET AUTHORITY

The Role of a Capital Market Authority

The primary role of a Capital Market Authority is to ensure that capital markets within its jurisdiction are properly functioning and that investors are adequately protected. This includes the oversight, licensing and regulation of securities exchanges and service providers, including broker-dealers and investment advisors. A Capital Market Authority must also monitor all transactions on markets within its jurisdiction in order to detect any potential irregularities or signs of market manipulation. Furthermore, it must promote investor education by providing guidance regarding investing practices as well as ensuring adequate disclosure standards for companies listed on exchanges. Additionally, it should be active in promoting good corporate governance practices among firms operating in its jurisdiction.

In order to fulfill these roles effectively, a Capital Market Authority may employ a range of regulatory tools such as setting minimum requirements for admission of companies onto exchanges, setting requirements for licensing and supervision of service providers, enforcing rules against insider trading, collecting data from regulated entities, conducting investigations into suspected violations, imposing fines where appropriate, issuing public warnings about risks associated with certain investments, and suspending or revoking licenses when necessary. By fulfilling these roles effectively, a Capital Market Authority helps ensure that capital markets within its jurisdiction are properly functioning and that investors are adequately protected.

The Responsibilities of a Capital Market Authority

1. A Capital Market Authority is responsible for registering and licensing capital market service providers. This includes overseeing the registration process to ensure that all service providers adhere to the relevant legal requirements, such as meeting capital adequacy standards and having in place appropriate internal controls. Furthermore, it must conduct

background checks on potential licensees to assess their suitability for engaging in securities-related activities. A Capital Market Authority also has a duty to monitor all registered entities closely in order to detect any irregularities or signs of misconduct. Finally, it is required to take action where necessary by suspending or revoking licenses when appropriate and issuing fines where warranted. By fulfilling these roles effectively, a Capital Market Authority helps ensure that investors receive adequate protection from fraudulent activity and market manipulation while maintaining fair and orderly markets within its jurisdiction.

2. A Capital Market Authority is responsible for registering and approving securities products, such as stocks, bonds, derivatives and other financial instruments. This involves ensuring that all products comply with applicable laws and regulations before they can be made available to the public. A Capital Market Authority also reviews prospectuses or offering documents to ensure that essential information about a product's terms and conditions are accurately disclosed. Furthermore, it must assess the risks associated with a product in order to determine whether the product is suitable for retail investors. Finally, it has the power to issue warnings if there are concerns over excessive risk-taking by issuers or market participants involved in trading activities related to a particular security. By fulfilling these roles effectively, a Capital Market Authority helps ensure an efficient flow of capital into productive investments while protecting investors from undue harm due to inadequate disclosure standards or faulty advice regarding risky investments.

3. A Capital Market Authority is responsible for regulating the marketing and sale of securities products. This includes setting minimum requirements for admission onto exchanges, enforcing rules against insider trading, collecting data from regulated entities, conducting investigations into suspected violations, issuing public warnings about risks associated with certain investments, imposing fines where appropriate, and suspending or revoking licenses when necessary. By fulfilling these roles effectively, a Capital Market Authority helps protect investors from fraudulent activity and market manipulation while making sure that only suitable financial products are available on exchanges within its jurisdiction.

4. A Capital Market Authority is responsible for inspecting and auditing securities firms within its jurisdiction. This includes conducting on-site examinations of firms in order to ensure that they are complying with applicable laws, regulations and corporate governance standards. Additionally, it must review financial statements and internal control mechanisms to assess the soundness of a firm's operations. A Capital Market Authority also has the power to impose sanctions or fines where appropriate if violations have been found. Furthermore, it can suspend or revoke licenses when necessary in order to protect investors from any potential harm due to misconduct or mismanagement by an entity operating in its jurisdiction. By fulfilling these roles effectively, a Capital Market Authority helps ensure that

all entities engaged in securities activities within its jurisdiction are functioning properly and providing adequate protection for investors' funds.

A Capital Market Authority is also responsible for ensuring that audit reports provided by external auditors meet professional standards as well as ensuring compliance with relevant legal requirements such as accounting rules and disclosure regimes pertaining to public offerings of securities products. In this regard, a Capital Market Authority must regularly examine audit reports submitted by registered entities, investigate complaints regarding alleged irregularities, perform surprise inspections of certified auditors working with listed companies, take action against auditors who fail to adhere to best practices, and provide guidance on proper auditing procedures for both domestic and foreign firms operating within its jurisdiction. By fulfilling these roles effectively, a Capital Market Authority helps promote good corporate governance among listed companies while protecting investors from fraud or misrepresentation through accurate reporting on company performance information disclosed through regular filings with exchanges it oversees.

5. A Capital Market Authority is responsible for investigating and prosecuting securities fraud. This includes reviewing complaints from investors, conducting on-site examinations of companies suspected of engaging in fraudulent activities, and collaborating with other law enforcement agencies both domestically and internationally to identify perpetrators. A Capital Market Authority has the power to issue formal warnings, impose fines or sanctions against violators, suspend or revoke licenses where appropriate, refer cases to criminal courts when necessary, and make public announcements about investigations into suspicious activities. Furthermore, it must work closely with other regulators in order to coordinate a comprehensive approach towards addressing market abuse. By fulfilling these roles effectively, a Capital Market Authority helps protect investors from false information or manipulation by ensuring that all entities engaged in securities activities within its jurisdiction are playing by the rules.

6. A Capital Market Authority is responsible for promoting investor education in order to ensure that individuals are well-informed when it comes to investing their money. A Capital Market Authority should work hard at providing detailed information regarding different types of investment products available on exchanges under its supervision through seminars conducted throughout its jurisdiction as well as via websites. Furthermore, it should provide guidance and advice to potential investors about how best to protect themselves when trading securities products by emphasizing the importance of understanding financial statements, researching companies and markets thoroughly before making any commitments, and familiarizing oneself with the risks associated with various investments. By educating investors on how best to protect themselves against irresponsible behavior from issuers and service providers looking only after their own interests instead of those of their customers', a

Capital Market Authority helps promote an efficient flow of capital into productive investments while protecting retail investors from harm due to inadequate disclosure standards or faulty advice regarding risky investments.

In addition to providing educational tools such as brochures, a Capital Market Authority is expected to enforce strict regulations pertaining to corporate governance standards along with stringent sanctions designed to deter fraudulent activities within its jurisdiction. Through public announcements detailing investigations into suspicious activity or fines imposed against violators, a Capital Market Authority sends a clear message that misconduct will not be tolerated while helping instill confidence amongst potential investors in relation to investing money into financial markets overseen by it. By fulfilling these roles effectively, a Capital Market Authority helps ensure that all entities engaged in securities activities within its jurisdiction are functioning properly and providing adequate protection for investors' funds while promoting a healthy culture of transparency where both listed companies and individual traders feel secure when taking part in market transactions.

Conclusion

A Capital Market Authority plays an integral role in ensuring that investment and securities markets are secure, accessible, and efficient. Through a commitment to promoting investor education, monitoring securities firms, supervising service providers, registering products, and addressing fraud and abuse, a Capital Market Authority is expected to protect investors' interests while providing access to capital markets.

CHAPTER III

ESTABLISHING A SUCCESSFUL STOCK EXCHANGE

A stock exchange is a financial institution or marketplace that facilitates the buying and selling of securities, such as stocks and bonds. It provides a platform for traders to buy and sell securities in an orderly manner, with the aim of maximizing profits from price changes. Setting up a successful stock exchange environment requires developing trading strategies, establishing partnerships with clearing houses and market makers, creating a secure environment, and meeting regulatory requirements. The benefits of setting up a successful stock exchange include increased liquidity within the market due to higher volumes of trades being made available on one platform; improved access to capital markets which allows investors to diversify their investments; more efficient pricing mechanisms due to greater transparency; lower transaction costs due to more competition among brokers; better risk management tools that allow traders to manage their positions more effectively; and improved customer service through faster settlement times.

Developing an Exchange Strategy

Developing a strategy for an exchange involves determining which products will be traded on the exchange and creating rules and regulations that govern how those trades will take place. Once these decisions have been made, it is time to create a trading platform that meets both regulatory requirements and provides traders with efficient access to the desired securities. The design of an effective system should include features such as real-time data feeds from different global markets, comprehensive risk management tools, fast execution speeds, user customizable order types, secure authentication processes, advanced charting capabilities, and customer service support when needed.

Establishing Partnerships

Once the trading platform is up and running, establishing partnerships with clearing houses, market makers, and stockbrokers can be essential in ensuring a successful stock exchange environment. A reliable clearinghouse is responsible for matching buyers and sellers within the exchange as well as settling trades quickly and efficiently without delay or risk of fraud. Market makers provide liquidity to the exchange by entering orders which help to create a more competitive environment within the system. Building relationships with multiple market makers will also encourage competition among them resulting in tighter spreads on securities being traded on the exchange. Finally, securing agreements with reputable stockbrokers can provide an additional layer of safety for investors since it ensures that all transactions meet regulatory requirements set forth by governing bodies. This helps protect both traders and brokers alike from potential issues caused by rogue actors or fraudulent operations within the marketplace. Overall, developing strong partnerships between these various stakeholders is critical in creating a secure and profitable environment for any type of investor looking to trade stocks or bonds through an established stock exchange platform.

Creating a Secure Exchange Environment

Creating a secure environment is essential for any successful stock exchange platform. This means ensuring that the system has adequate security measures in place such as firewalls, encryption protocols, and multi-factor authentication to protect traders from cyberattacks or fraud. Additionally, procedures must be put in place to monitor user activity so that any suspicious trades can be flagged and investigated quickly before significant damage is done. Furthermore, it is important for the trading platform to have up-to-date compliance policies in order to meet regulatory requirements set forth by governing bodies.

Building an efficient management system is also key when setting up a stock exchange platform. This involves developing data models which allow investors to track relevant information such as market conditions and trends over time; creating robust algorithms which generate trading signals based on this data; creating order entry systems which execute trades according to these signals; and offering advanced tools such as risk management solutions which help investors minimize losses while maximizing potential gains from their positions within the market. All of these components have to work together harmoniously so that traders have access to all of the resources necessary for making informed decisions about their investment portfolios quickly and accurately without excessive delays or errors occurring along the way.

Finally, developing customer service protocols is critical when operating a successful stock exchange environment since satisfied customers will come back again if they receive prompt responses whenever they need assistance with something related to their accounts or transactions on the platform. To ensure quality customer support services, exchanges should invest in staff training programs so that agents are well equipped with knowledge regarding various aspects of securities trading including understanding different types of orders, financial markets terminology, and market risks associated with investing strategies.

Regulatory Requirements

Once the necessary licenses are secured, it is essential to ensure that all regulatory requirements are met. This involves familiarizing oneself with the specific regulations set forth by governing bodies in order to comply with their standards and filing any applicable reports accordingly. It can also involve establishing internal policies which go above and beyond what is required of them in order to guarantee a secure trading environment for customers. For example, these could include measures such as setting daily transaction limits for individual accounts, implementing Know Your Customer/ Anti-Money Laundering procedures when opening new accounts, or maintaining records of customer activity on the exchange platform in case of audit inquiries from regulatory agencies.

Additionally, exchanges should take steps to protect themselves from potential legal action against them due to non-compliance with regulations or misconduct within their operations. Having robust legal counsel available who is knowledgeable about financial securities markets can be invaluable in this area since they will have a better understanding of how rules and laws apply specifically within an exchange context and can help provide guidance on how best to proceed whenever questions arise regarding certain aspects related to running a successful stock exchange platform.

Finally, having strong relationships with other stakeholders involved in the industry such as clearing houses, market makers and brokers are also beneficial since they may be able to offer additional insight into meeting regulatory requirements while providing support during compliance audits if needed.

Conclusion

Setting up a successful stock exchange platform requires careful planning and preparation. Taking the time to familiarize oneself with the relevant regulatory requirements and implementing advanced security measures are essential for creating a safe environment that users can trust when conducting their transactions on the platform. Additionally, developing an efficient management system which allows investors to access real-time data while also providing them with tools such as automated trading signals helps traders make more informed decisions about their investment portfolios quickly and accurately. Furthermore, investing in customer service protocols so that agents are knowledgeable about different aspects of securities trading will help ensure customers receive prompt assistance whenever they need it. When all of these components come together harmoniously, it is possible for exchanges to create lasting value by offering a secure trading environment where customers have access to all necessary resources needed for making sound financial decisions without any undue delays or errors occurring along the way.

CHAPTER IV

CAPITAL MARKET SERVICE PROVIDERS

Capital market service providers are professionals that provide specialized services, such as investment banking, portfolio management and securities brokerage to companies, investors and other financial institutions. Capital market service providers play a vital role in the efficient functioning of capital markets by acting as intermediaries between buyers and sellers of financial securities and providing expert advice to help their clients make sound financial decisions.

The benefits of working with capital market service providers are many; they help companies access a wide variety of capital sources through initial and secondary offerings of securities, create efficient and effective capital structures, execute financial transactions, negotiate mergers and acquisitions, maximize returns through strategic investments, reduce risk by managing clients' portfolios and ensure compliance with laws and regulations.

Capital market service providers include:

Investment banks specialize in underwriting new securities offerings and raising money for companies through public offerings or private placements. They also provide advice on mergers and acquisitions as well as corporate restructuring activities like buybacks or spin-offs. Investment banks typically offer services in underwriting, sales and trading, corporate restructuring, corporate finance advisory services, research analysis, structured finance and portfolio management.

Investment advisors help individuals manage their investments in stocks, bonds, mutual funds and other securities. They provide tailored advice based on an individual's risk tolerance level, goals and objectives for specific investments.

Portfolio managers work with institutional investors and high-net-worth individuals in developing and managing customized portfolios based on their clients' risk tolerance levels and long-term objectives in order to maximize returns while minimizing volatility associated with investments. Portfolio managers also offer advice on various asset classes such as stocks, bonds or derivatives depending on what is most appropriate given the clients' needs.

Brokerage firms specialize in buying and selling securities such as stocks or bonds for clients either through direct transactions or through exchanges and other trading platforms. Brokerage firms typically charge commissions based off each transaction they facilitate. In addition to helping investors purchase and sell securities, brokerage firms provide services such as margin lending and portfolio management.

Custodians are financial institutions that hold and safeguard clients' assets, usually in the form of stocks, bonds, collective investment schemes, and other securities. They also execute trading orders from their clients based upon given instructions and ensure accurate records are kept regarding all transactions.

Conclusion

Capital market service providers play a vital role in the efficient functioning of capital markets by helping investors make informed decisions based on sound advice and research, while also providing them with the assurance that their investments are managed in accordance with applicable laws and regulations. Capital market service providers also give companies easier access to larger pools of potential investors while providing them the support needed when raising funds or going through corporate restructuring. Whether it be obtaining financing for new ventures and expansions, diversifying portfolios through strategic investments or navigating complex merger and acquisition transactions, capital market service providers have the experience and knowledge necessary to help make these processes smoother and more successful.

CHAPTER V

CREDIT RATING AGENCIES

Credit rating agencies are capital market service providers that play an influential role in the proper functioning of capital markets. They are organizations that provide independent evaluations of the creditworthiness of various entities such as government bonds, corporate debt, and other financial instruments. These ratings determine the likelihood that an issuer will be able to repay a loan or fulfill its obligations in regards to the instrument being rated. Credit rating agencies play a vital role in financial markets by providing investors with objective and factual information about potential investments which can help inform decision-making processes. Rating organizations offer insight into investment risks, helping buyers evaluate whether they should invest their money or not. The ratings also help banks decide on how much capital is needed for certain loans and investments so that they can remain adequately protected against defaulting borrowers. In addition to providing assessments of risk levels, credit rating agencies are also responsible for monitoring changes within an organization's credit profile over time, thus allowing investors to adjust their portfolios accordingly.

Credit rating agencies are typically divided into two different categories: national and international credit rating agencies. National credit rating agencies usually provide ratings for entities within their specific countries, while international ones, such as Standard & Poor's, Moody's and Fitch Ratings cover both domestic as well as foreign investments across the globe. Ratings from these organizations range from AAA (the highest) to D (the lowest).

The process used to determine ratings is highly complex and involves detailed analysis from experts within the industry. Credit rating agencies rely on both quantitative and qualitative methods to evaluate potential investments and assign ratings accordingly. This process includes evaluating historical data about the issuer including analyzing factors such as cash flow ratios, leverage levels, and liquidity metrics. It also involves analyzing trends within an issuer's industry, conducting interviews with company representatives and other stakeholders, along with reviewing legal documents related to any transactions conducted by the entity in question. Once all relevant information has been gathered and analyzed thoroughly, a final rating is assigned based on this assessment which can then be used by investors when making decisions regarding potential investments they may wish to pursue.

Conclusion

Credit rating agencies play an important role in capital markets, providing market participants with independent assessments of creditworthiness and risk of securities and issuers. By providing investors with a concise summary of an issuer's ability to meet its obligations, rating agencies help reduce systemic risk and improve capital market efficiency.

CHAPTER VI

CAPITAL MARKET SECURITIES

Capital market securities are financial instruments that are issued by corporations and governments to raise capital. These securities can be in the form of debt securities, equity securities and derivatives. Capital market securities give investors the opportunity to build wealth over time by investing in diversified assets and earning returns on those investments.

Debt Securities

Debt securities are fixed-income instruments such as bonds that provide the holder with a predetermined stream of payments over a certain period. Debt securities are generally issued by governments and corporations in order to raise capital for projects or operations. Debt securities can be either short-term (maturing within one year) or long-term (maturing beyond one year). Common types of debt securities include government bonds, corporate bonds, and asset-backed securities. Debt security holders have priority over equity holders if there is ever a situation where creditors must be paid first in order for debts to be settled (during market downturns or bankruptcies). When investing in debt securities it is important for investors to consider various factors, such as credit ratings (which measure how likely an issuer is able to pay back its obligations), yield spreads (differences between what a bond pays versus similar investment grade bonds) and duration (the length of time until full repayment).

Government bonds are debt obligations issued by governments to fund public projects such as schools, roads, bridges, and hospitals as well as to supplement government budget. In most countries, these types of investments offer tax benefits to investors since the interest earned is exempt from federal taxes. However, it is important to note that government bonds tend to have lower returns compared with other investments due to their low-risk nature.

Corporate bonds are debt securities issued by companies to raise capital for projects or operations. They generally offer higher yields than government bonds but carry greater risks since the issuer is a private entity and not backed by the government.

Asset-backed securities (ABS) are financial instruments backed by specific assets such as mortgages, auto loans and credit card receivables, and provide monthly cash flows when payments on those underlying assets are received. ABS typically come with higher yields than traditional fixed-income investments because they involve greater risk due to their dependence on principal repayment performance of underlying assets.

Equity Securities

Equity securities are capital market securities that represent ownership stake in a company. Equity security holders are referred to as shareholders or stockholders, and have the right to vote on certain matters and decisions regarding how the company is run, receive dividends from profits, and share in any capital gains should the value of their shares increase. Investing in equity offers potential for growth through appreciation of underlying assets and dividends paid out by issuers when profits exceed expenses. However, this also involves greater risk than debt securities since there is no guarantee that returns will be realized due to market volatility or changes in issuer performance.

Common stock is the most common form of equity security and represents an ownership stake in a company. Common stockholders are able to vote on certain matters related to how the company is run (electing board members, approving mergers and acquisitions, setting executive compensation packages), and may receive dividends from profits. When the market value of their shares increases, they also share in any capital gains that result.

Preferred stock is another type of equity security that gives holders priority over common shareholders if the company were to liquidate or go bankrupt. They typically do not have voting rights but instead offer fixed dividend payments with higher yields than those offered by common stocks. Additionally, preferred stockholders may have an option to convert their shares into common stock at a specified price at a future date.

Overall, investing in equity securities provides investors with access to high-growth opportunities while still allowing them to diversify away from more traditional assets such as fixed-income instruments; this makes them ideal for those looking for higher returns or who want exposure to industries where growth prospects appear promising.

Derivative Securities

Derivative securities are financial instruments that derive their value from an underlying asset, such as a stock, bond, commodity or currency. Investors use derivatives to hedge against risk and speculate on the direction of price movements in markets. Derivatives allow investors to leverage their investments by taking larger positions than they would otherwise be able to with just cash.

This increased leverage can generate higher returns from smaller investments but also carries greater risks of losses.

Options are derivatives that give the buyer (holder) the right, but not the obligation, to buy or sell an underlying asset at a set strike price before an expiration date. Options offer investors flexibility and control over their investments because they can choose how much of their money is exposed at any given time depending on whether they decide to exercise their option or let it expire worthless. This makes options attractive hedging instruments when used correctly since buyers have limited downside risks while still being able to leverage potential profits from market movements in favor of their position.

Futures are derivative contracts that obligate parties to buy or sell a certain asset at a pre-determined price on a specified date in the future. Futures provide investors with a way to manage price risk by allowing them to lock in prices for commodities, currencies and securities that may be volatile or difficult to predict. They can also be used as an effective tool for speculation as they allow traders to take positions on various assets without having to actually purchase them outright.

Forwards are similar in nature compared with futures but differ mainly due to their customizability; forwards contracts have more flexible terms than standard futures, including customizable delivery dates, settlement methods and payment schedules which make them ideal for companies seeking tailored agreements between themselves and other parties involved in transactions such as currency trades or commodity purchases and sales.

Swaps are derivative contracts between two parties to exchange one financial asset or obligation for another. Swaps involve the simultaneous purchase and sale of a set of cash flows from two different parties, oftentimes at different prices. Swaps allow each party to gain exposure to the desired market without having to own the underlying security or instrument itself. The most common types of swaps are interest rate swaps, currency swaps, and commodity swaps.

Conclusion

Capital market securities offer a variety of opportunities for investors to diversify and grow their portfolios. Debt securities provide investors with steady income while also providing some protection from volatility due to their fixed nature. Equity investments come with potentially higher returns compared to debt securities and are ideal for those looking for exposure to high-growth industries or seeking an additional layer of diversification within their portfolio. Derivatives offer numerous benefits in terms of hedging risk and providing access to certain asset classes otherwise unattainable through traditional investment methods alone. Ultimately it is important that individual investors carefully consider all options before making any decisions so they can select the best instruments suited towards meeting their long-term financial goals.

CHAPTER VII

INSTITUTIONAL INVESTORS

Institutional Investors are large financial institutions, such as pension funds, insurance companies and collective investment schemes that invest money on behalf of their clients. They are an important part of the global financial system, providing liquidity to markets and helping to ensure efficient capital allocation. Institutional investors play a key role by providing access to capital for businesses and investment opportunities for individuals. Institutional investors have become increasingly influential over time due to their size and ability to make substantial investments in public securities. Their presence can significantly impact stock prices as well as other aspects of the economy such as interest rates and currency exchange rates.

Types of Institutional Investors

Pension Funds are institutional investors that provide retirement benefits to their members. They typically invest in a variety of assets, including stocks and bonds. Pension funds generally have long-term investment goals and tend to be more conservative in their approach than other types of institutional investors. This is due to the fact that they need to ensure sufficient returns for their members over the long term in order to meet their obligations.

Insurance Companies are another type of institutional investor. These companies typically hold investments such as government bonds, equity securities and derivatives in order to generate income from interest payments or capital gains on those investments. Insurance companies also use these investments as a means of hedging against risks associated with providing insurance policies, such as death or disability benefits paid out by life insurance contracts or medical claims incurred through health plans.

Collective Investment Schemes are professionally managed portfolios consisting of pooled investor money invested into different asset classes such as stocks and bonds. Collective investment schemes can either be actively managed or passively indexed depending upon the fund's objectives.

Hedge Funds are private investment partnerships created specifically for wealthy individuals seeking higher returns than what public markets offer along with greater control over how their money is being invested compared to traditional collective investment schemes.

Endowments refer to large sums of money held by organizations dedicated towards charitable causes or educational institutions used for funding scholarships, research programs and buildings. Endowments may include donations received from individuals but generally consist mainly of larger contributions made by businesses which benefit from tax deductions associated with endowed gifts.

Benefits of Working with Institutional Investors

Institutional investors offer a number of advantages to businesses looking for capital or investment opportunities. Access to capital is one of the primary benefits as institutional investors have the ability to provide large amounts of money quickly, allowing companies to expand their operations and pursue new projects. Additionally, these investors often bring with them a wealth of expertise in financial markets which can be invaluable when making decisions on investments; they also typically have access to resources such as research teams and industry contacts that smaller firms may not possess. Moreover, institutional investors are usually able to secure more favorable terms than what an individual investor could achieve on their own due to economies of scale, meaning businesses can benefit from lower costs associated with financing deals. Finally, working with institutional investors allows for greater risk mitigation through diversification since funds can be spread out across multiple asset classes or industries thereby reducing exposure if any particular sector experiences significant losses.

Conclusion

Working with institutional investors has significant benefits to businesses and investors alike. Access to capital is one of the main advantages as these firms typically have large amounts of money readily available for investments; additionally, their expertise in financial markets along with access to resources such as research teams and industry contacts provide invaluable insight when considering potential investment opportunities. Furthermore, businesses can benefit from more favourable terms than what an individual investor could achieve on their own due to economies of scale offered by larger funds. In conclusion, working with institutional investors can provide long-term returns that offer positive outcomes both financially as well as strategically for all parties involved.

CHAPTER VIII

COLLECTIVE INVESTMENT SCHEMES

Collective investment schemes are investment vehicles designed to pool the money of many different investors and invest it in a variety of assets such as stocks, bonds, and other securities. These schemes are managed by professional teams of financial experts who are responsible for researching, selecting, monitoring, and adjusting investments according to predetermined objectives (income or capital appreciation).

Collective investment schemes are becoming increasingly popular as a result of their numerous advantages. The primary advantage of investing in collective investment schemes is that they allow individual investors to gain access to the same types of investments and strategies typically only available to large institutional investors with significant resources. As such, many individuals are able to diversify their portfolios and gain exposure to different markets without having to invest large amounts of capital into each security. Furthermore, professional management is available when investing in collective investment schemes which enables efficient operation and reduces risks associated with less experienced individual investors. Additionally, due to the economies of scale associated with these large pools of funds, they often offer lower fees and better returns than traditional investments. All these combined make collective investment schemes an attractive option for many looking to increase their financial portfolio's potential return while minimizing risk exposure at the same time.

Types of Collective Investment Schemes

There are several types of collective investment schemes available, but the two major ones are open-ended collective investment schemes and closed-ended collective investment schemes.

Open-ended collective investment schemes allow investors to buy and sell shares in the scheme at any time, and the value of the shares is determined by the net asset value of the underlying securities that make up the portfolio. These schemes have no fixed size, meaning the fund manager can create or redeem shares in line with market conditions and investor demand. This allows for more flexibility and liquidity for investors as well as greater opportunities for diversification within the portfolio.

Closed-ended collective investment schemes issue a limited number of shares on an initial public offering basis and trade the shares freely on exchanges like stocks. Unlike open-ended schemes, which can create or redeem shares in line with investor demand, closed-ended funds have fixed portfolios and offer investors the ability to buy and sell their holdings based on market prices on an exchange. This allows for more control over the timing of investments as well as greater liquidity than open-ended collective investment schemes.

Other collective investment schemes include **Exchange Traded Funds (ETFs)**, which are similar to open-ended collective investment schemes but they can be traded on an exchange like stocks and provide additional liquidity; **Hedge Funds** and **Private Equity Funds**, which offer more aggressive investment strategies that may involve higher risk, but also greater returns if successfully executed; and **Venture Capital Funds**, which target early-stage companies with high growth potential for long-term capital appreciation opportunities.

Collective Investment Schemes can also be categorized based on their investment policies. **Equity Funds** invest mainly in stocks and aim to provide capital growth over the long term. **Bond Funds** invest mainly in bonds issued by corporations and government entities, and focus on providing steady income as well as capital appreciation. **Money Market Funds** typically invest in short-term debt instruments such as treasury bills and certificates of deposit. **Balanced Funds** combine stocks and bonds, usually through investing into a mix of both equity and fixed-income securities but generally maintain an even ratio between them which provides stability against market risks while still allowing for potential profit-earning opportunities. **Index Funds** seek to replicate the performance of a specific benchmark index such as S&P 500 or FTSE 100; these funds tend to have lower management fees due to their passive nature.

Conclusion

Collective investment schemes are an increasingly popular form of investing due to the range of benefits associated with them, including greater diversification, professional management, increased liquidity, access to a wide range of assets, and lower fees than other individual investments. It is important for potential investors to become informed about collective investment schemes in order to make better decisions about how and where to allocate their money to maximize returns without taking on too much risk or sacrificing too much liquidity.

CHAPTER IX

SECURITIES CLEARING AND SETTLEMENT

Securities Clearing and Settlement is an essential component of the operations of any capital market, providing a secure, transparent and efficient way for buyers and sellers of securities (such as stocks and bonds) to complete transactions. Securities clearing and settlement is the process of finalizing a securities transaction. It involves transferring ownership of a security from one party to another in exchange for payment, ensuring that all relevant financial obligations are met. The entire process starts when an order to buy or sell securities is placed with a broker and ends when funds are transferred between parties' accounts.

Securities clearing and settlement involves two distinct steps: **clearing**, which establishes who owns the assets; and **settlement**, which ensures that payment for these assets is made. The participants in this process are numerous, including brokers, market makers, central counterparty clearers, custodians and depositary banks. **Brokers** act on behalf of their clients to buy or sell securities while **market makers** provide liquidity by buying and selling securities at prices they set themselves. **Central counterparties** provide a guarantee between buyers and sellers so that if either party defaults on its obligations then the central counterparty will step in to ensure settlement takes place. **Custodians** and **depositary banks** hold investors' securities and cash deposits until needed for trading purposes and act as intermediaries between buyers and sellers during transactions.

The clearing process involves several different steps, including verifying the identities of buyers and sellers, executing trades on behalf of clients and obtaining settlement instructions from buyers/sellers involved in each transaction, checking documents related to transfers such as share certificates or stock transfer forms against any outstanding offers or bids prior to execution, and ensuring accuracy by cross-referencing data provided by various sources so that only legitimate transactions take place.

The settlement process is the final step in completing a securities transaction. This is when the ownership of the security is transferred from one party to another and payment for the securities is made. The transfer of ownership can be accomplished either through physical delivery (the actual stock certificates are exchanged) or book entry (an electronic record of ownership). When settling securities it is important that they are delivered correctly according to contract terms. Physical delivery requires that stocks must be registered under the name of the buyer before being transferred while book-entry transactions involve transferring shares electronically through a central depository. These steps ensure accuracy and avoid any disputes over who owns what after a trade has taken place.

Risks

Operational risk can arise in the process of clearing and settling securities due to incorrect or incomplete documentation, processing errors, or other mistakes made by market participants. These types of errors can lead to delays in settlement, missed deadlines or even failed trades. To mitigate these risks, it is important that all parties involved take measures such as implementing automated systems for processing high-volume transactions and having a backup system in place should one fail. Additionally, processes must be put into place to ensure accurate data entry and verification with strict procedures surrounding the handling of sensitive information.

Counterparty risk is the risk associated with one party not performing according to contractual obligations during a transaction. This can occur when either side fails to settle their end of the deal on time, resulting in losses for both parties involved but especially for those who had already provided funds before being let down by their counterparties' inability (or unwillingness) to fulfill their part of the agreement. To minimize this type of risk, it is essential that clearing agents thoroughly check out potential counterparties before entering into any contract with them and verify documents related to each transaction are correct before execution takes place.

Settlement risk occurs when there is a delay between two parties exchanging assets during a transaction which leads one side to incurring losses if prices move against them while they wait for payment/ delivery completion from their counterparty. To reduce this type of exposure, trading institutions may choose to implement guarantees such as those offered by central counterparties which provide assurance that settlements will go through even if one side defaults on its obligations thus protecting investors from unnecessary financial losses due to unforeseen circumstances.

Liquidity risk arises when an investor does not have sufficient funds available at short notice needed for making payments/ settlements upon trade execution leading them unable to complete orders placed upon markets. This risk can be mitigated by central counterparties that provide liquidity for investors who may not be able to immediately provide funds.

Conclusion

Securities clearing and settlement is an essential part of capital markets that allows market participants to safely and efficiently complete transactions. The role of brokers, market makers, central counterparties, custodians and depository banks are all integral components in ensuring that trades are cleared and settled correctly according to contractual agreements. Additionally, these entities help mitigate operational risks like processing errors by adopting strict procedures around data entry verification. Finally, they also play a vital role in mitigating counterparty risks through extensive background checks before entering into agreements while also minimizing settlement risk and liquidity risk exposures using guarantees provided by central counterparties.

CHAPTER X

SECURITY DEMATERIALIZATION

Security dematerialization is the process of transforming physical securities (such as share certificates) into electronic records. In its most basic form, security dematerialization involves creating digital records or certificates in place of traditional paper-based documents related to ownership of a particular asset. These digital records are then stored securely on computer systems and networks that can be accessed remotely via secure networks.

One of the primary benefits associated with security dematerialization is efficient security ownership management. By creating digital records in place of traditional paper-based documents, it becomes easier to track and update ownership information quickly in response to market fluctuations. This allows investors to accurately maintain their portfolio even under changing market conditions, resulting in improved decision-making and increased returns on investments.

Another benefit of security dematerialization is reduced cost and fraud risk associated with physical storage and handling of paperwork. By eliminating cumbersome paperwork related to transactions, financial institutions are able to reduce costs related to fraud prevention as well as time taken for settlement processes significantly which further enhances overall efficiency levels across markets. Additionally, authentication measures implemented at various stages throughout the entire transaction process help protect confidential data from being accessed by unauthorized parties while providing an additional layer of protection against fraudulent activities that could occur if physical documents were used instead.

In addition to these advantages, using electronic securities increases liquidity across capital markets due to faster settlement times compared with manual processing methods which require lengthy confirmation procedures between each trading party involved in a transaction. This can result in more profitable opportunities for traders who are able to take advantage of rapidly changing prices within shorter periods when dealing with assets such as stocks where price movements can be swift due to rapid buying/ selling activity from large numbers of participants.

Challenges of Security Dematerialization

Data integration is one of the major challenges associated with security dematerialization. This refers to the difficulty in connecting disparate systems and databases that are used by different financial institutions and investors while attempting to execute a transaction or transfer ownership records electronically. If these components are not properly integrated, it can lead to errors occurring during processing transactions which could potentially result in losses for both parties involved as well as lower overall efficiency levels across capital markets.

Additionally, security and privacy concerns remain paramount when dealing with digital securities since confidential data-related transactions must be kept safe from unauthorized access at all times. Authentication measures implemented throughout the entire process help protect sensitive information from being obtained by criminals but there still remains the risk of hacking attacks which could potentially compromise the integrity of the system if not dealt with promptly.

Conclusion

Security dematerialization has revolutionized the way financial transactions are conducted and ownership records maintained within capital markets. By creating digital representations of paper-based securities, it has become easier for investors to manage their portfolios efficiently while reducing costs associated with paperwork handling and storage. Additionally, security measures implemented at various stages throughout the entire process help protect confidential data from falling into wrong hands thus minimizing potential risks related to fraud or theft. However, there still remains numerous challenges that need to be addressed such as ensuring proper data integration between different systems and databases, and deploying strong encryption protocols to mitigate any possible threats posed by unauthorized individuals.

CHAPTER XI

FINANCIAL CRIMES

Financial crimes pose serious threats to capital markets and economies. They can range from fraud, identity theft and cybercrime to insider trading, money laundering and embezzlement. Financial crimes have become increasingly sophisticated due to the growth of technology and globalization. These types of criminal activities often target vulnerable individuals, businesses and government entities in order to access funds illegally without detection. Financial crimes can be committed by those with direct knowledge of a company's finances as well as those outside the organization who use deception or manipulation for their own gain. While some financial criminals may operate alone, many times they will work together with others in organized crime rings or even within legitimate organizations that lack proper oversight measures in place.

Money laundering is the process of creating a complex trail of financial transactions in order to conceal the source and ultimate destination of funds. This type of criminal activity can involve transferring money through offshore accounts or multiple companies, falsifying invoices and other documents, disguising how funds were obtained and using legitimate businesses as fronts for illegal activities. Money laundering allows criminals to hide their profits from tax authorities while also enabling them to move large sums without detection.

Insider trading is a type of financial crime where an individual uses information not available publicly to purchase or sell securities before such information is made public. The insider may use this confidential knowledge for their own benefit instead of sharing it with others who could potentially benefit from such knowledge. Insider trading can have serious repercussions for those involved as it has been known to destabilize markets by creating artificial price fluctuations that are not reflective of true market conditions.

Fraud involves intentionally deceiving someone in order to gain something at their expense, usually money or property. Common types include identity theft and investment fraud. Fraudsters use various methods including false accounting records, impersonation schemes and cyber attacks in order to access private data which they then use for their own gain.

Compliance and Regulation

AML (Anti-Money Laundering) regulations help prevent, detect and report financial crimes such as money laundering. These laws require financial institutions to take steps such as identity verification of customers, monitoring transactions for suspicious activity and reporting any suspected criminal activity to the appropriate authorities.

KYC (Know Your Customer) is another compliance instrument that seeks to protect businesses from fraud by verifying customer identities before conducting a transaction or opening an account. This helps reduce the potential risk of illegal activities being conducted through false identities or misrepresented information. KYC requirements usually include collecting proof of identity documents, validating them against reliable sources and regularly reviewing customer accounts/ transactions for any suspicious behavior or changes in personal information provided at time of onboarding.

Prevention and Detection

Data analysis is an important tool in the prevention and detection of financial crimes. By analyzing large sets of data, patterns can be identified that indicate suspicious activity or fraud. Advanced analytics such as machine learning are being used to detect fraudulent behavior more quickly and accurately than ever before. Data analysis also allows for the identification of potential risks before they become a problem which helps in preventing future incidents from occurring.

Technology solutions have made it easier for organizations to monitor their finances and identify discrepancies or red flags that may indicate criminal activities taking place. These include automated systems for tracking transactions, user authentication methods and advanced encryption techniques to keep information secure. All these measures help ensure compliance with anti-money laundering regulations while also providing a greater level of protection against financial crime.

Auditing is another effective way to prevent and detect financial crimes by ensuring all processes are operating within accepted standards set out by regulatory bodies. Audits provide an independent assessment of internal controls which can uncover any weaknesses or irregularities that could lead to frauds committed by employees or external parties alike. Companies should ensure regular audits take place on their books in order to safeguard themselves from potential losses due to criminal activities taking place undetected within their organizations.

Conclusion

Financial crimes such as money laundering, insider trading and fraud are serious threats to capital markets and economies. To combat these activities, businesses must ensure they adhere to compliance requirements such as AML/KYC standards and take steps to protect customer data by implementing technology solutions. Finally, auditing is an important tool which helps companies identify any discrepancies or irregularities that may be indicative of criminal behavior within their organization. By taking all necessary measures to protect themselves from financial crime, businesses can reduce the risk posed by fraudulent activities while ensuring a safe environment for investors and customers alike.

CHAPTER XII

CORPORATE GOVERNANCE

Corporate governance refers to the system of rules, practices, and processes used by a company to ensure that its operations are conducted in a fair and ethical manner. Corporate governance is essentially about making sure that companies act responsibly towards their stakeholders, including shareholders, customers, employees, suppliers and the communities in which they operate. Having strong corporate governance systems in place can help increase investor confidence in a company's management team, protect stakeholders' interests, promote long-term value creation for companies' owners, improve overall financial performance within organizations and reduce risks associated with unethical behavior. Additionally, it helps protect against fraudulent activities such as insider trading or accounting irregularities, which can have serious consequences for both investors and the public at large. By implementing effective corporate governance policies, organizations can ensure that all stakeholders benefit from their business operations while also reducing potential risks associated with mismanagement or unethical practices.

Components of Effective Corporate Governance

Board of Directors

The board of directors is a critical component of corporate governance and plays a key role in the success of any organization. The board's primary duty is to oversee the management, financial performance and strategic direction of a company. More specifically, it is responsible for setting strategic goals, developing policies that guide management decisions, and ensuring compliance with applicable laws and regulations. The board is also responsible for appointing executive officers, establishing objectives for executive leadership and evaluating their performance, monitoring risks, approving major corporate transactions such as mergers and acquisitions as well as ensuring proper disclosure policies are in place so that shareholders have access to accurate information about their investments. By acting as an independent body representing all stakeholders within an organization, the board helps build trust between executives and shareholders while creating long-term value for the company.

Shareholder Rights

Shareholder rights are an important part of corporate governance, as they ensure that the interests of shareholders are represented in a company's decisions. Shareholders have invested their money into the organization, and thus enjoy the right to vote on major matters at shareholder meetings, including board of director elections, executive compensation packages, proposed mergers and acquisition approvals as well as changes to the company's structure or bylaws. Having voting rights allows shareholders to have a say in how their investments are managed and ensure that their voices will be heard when it comes to making important decisions about the future direction of the business.

Another key shareholder right is access to financial information regarding the performance of their investments. Companies must provide investors with accurate information so that they can make informed decisions about their holdings. This includes providing regular updates on financial performance, dividends paid out over time, and debt levels. It also involves offering transparency into board decision-making processes so that shareholders can understand why certain actions were taken and which strategies have been implemented for growth or cost savings purposes. By having access to such information, investors can evaluate whether they feel comfortable continuing with their current level of involvement or if there might be more profitable opportunities elsewhere.

Finally, shareholders should also have clear communication channels available in order for them to express any concerns directly with management teams.

The Management

The management of a company is another major component of corporate governance. Management is responsible for ensuring that all aspects of an organization's operations run smoothly and efficiently. This includes setting strategic goals, developing plans and budgets for achieving these objectives, leading the implementation of actions required and monitoring progress over time, hiring talented individuals with relevant skillsets as well as motivating existing employees through recognition or rewards when they excel at their tasks. Good management practices enable organizations to reach greater heights by maximizing efficiency levels thus increasing returns for all stakeholders.

Transparency and Disclosure

Transparency and disclosure are essential components of corporate governance. Transparency refers to the availability of accurate and timely information that shareholders can access in order to understand how a company is performing and make informed decisions about their investments. Companies should provide shareholders with regular reports detailing financial performance, strategy updates or any other pertinent information related to business operations so they can evaluate the organization's progress over time. Additionally, companies should maintain open communication channels such as investor relations websites or shareholder meetings for shareholders to have direct access to executives and ask questions directly. Providing up-to-date information on all aspects of an organization's operations helps ensure trust between shareholders and management while reducing potential risks due to lack of knowledge or understanding from either party.

Audit

Audit is another essential component of a company's corporate governance system. It is important for companies to adhere to legal and regulatory frameworks in order to ensure accuracy and prevent any fraud or mismanagement from occurring. Audit provides an independent assessment of the organization's financial statements which helps protect investors from being misled by inaccurate information. The scope of the audit process should include reviewing internal controls, examining accounting records, verifying assets and liabilities as well as other procedures necessary to obtain reasonable assurance about whether the financial statements are free from material misstatement. Auditors also provide opinion on the fairness of the reported results based on their findings which helps stakeholders better understand a company's performance over time.

Risk Management

Risk management is another critical part of any company's corporate governance system, as it helps organizations identify, assess and manage potential risks in order to minimize their impact or eliminate them entirely. Through effective risk management practices, organizations can reduce potential losses from unforeseen events while improving overall performance over time. Companies should develop comprehensive risk management policies to ensure all areas of the business are monitored for potential threats and that proper procedures are in place to respond quickly if needed. This includes developing controls on financial reporting, investing activities and strategic decisions.

Other popular risk mitigation strategies include diversifying investments, purchasing insurance policies to protect against unforeseen events such as employee injury or property damage, and deploying contingency plans for how operations will continue if key personnel become unavailable due to illness, injury or death. By proactively managing risks within the organization, companies can protect their investments while creating long-term value for shareholders over time.

Internal Controls

Internal controls are yet another important element of corporate governance which involve policies and procedures put in place to ensure accurate information is captured, stored securely and reported accurately throughout an organization. Internal controls help mitigate operational risks by ensuring data integrity across all departments while providing a framework for monitoring adherence with laws and regulations governing business operations. Organizations should develop adequate internal control measures such as segregation of duties, access restrictions on sensitive data or resources and regular audits or reviews conducted by independent third parties to ensure reliable reporting processes are in place throughout the company's operations. By having robust internal control measures in place, organizations can build trust between shareholders and executives while reducing associated risks related to unethical behavior or mismanagement of funds over time.

Conclusion

Good corporate governance is essential for successful companies as it helps ensure accountability and transparency while mitigating risks related to unethical behavior or mismanagement of funds. Through effective corporate governance practices, organizations can build trust among stakeholders by providing accurate information on financial performance, policy changes or any other important matters affecting the company’s future direction. Additionally, implementing measures such as risk management policies, internal controls and transparent reporting processes can help mitigate potential losses over time while creating long-term value for shareholders. By taking a proactive approach to corporate governance, organizations can ensure their investments are secure while gaining assurance that all areas of operations are monitored appropriately at all times.

CHAPTER XIII

RISKS IN CAPITAL MARKETS

Capital markets are financial systems in which investors can buy and sell equities, bonds, and other securities. They provide a way for businesses to raise equity and debt capital for operations or investments. With the potential rewards come risks associated with investing in these markets. Capital market risk is defined as the possibility of an investment's return not meeting expectations due to changes in economic conditions such as interest rates or political events like wars or elections. There are several types of capital market risks that investors must be aware of before entering into any transaction. These include economic risks (such as interest rate risk, inflation risk, and exchange rate risk), credit risks (default risk and recovery risk), market & liquidity risks, political risk (political instability risk and regulatory changes risk), technological risk (cyber security & data security) and other risks (opportunity cost risk and legal risks).

Economic Risks

Economic risks are one of the most important types of capital market risks that investors must consider before entering into any transaction. **Interest rate risk** relates to the possibility that changes in interest rates may cause a change in an investment's return. **Inflation risk** is another key economic risk associated with investing and refers to the potential for rising prices to decrease purchasing power, leading to lower returns on investments over time. **Exchange rate risk** is also a major economic concern when it comes to capital markets as fluctuations in foreign currency exchange rates can significantly alter a portfolio's value. Lastly, there is **sovereign debt default risk** which occurs when governments fail or refuse to make payments on their outstanding debts.

Credit Risks

Credit risks refer to the possibility that an issuer of a debt instrument may not be able to make payments on time or in full. **Default risk** is the primary form of credit risk, which occurs when a borrower fails to pay back their loan or obligation in accordance with its terms. This can cause investors to suffer financial losses if they are unable to recover their principal amount plus any accrued interest or other benefits associated with the investment. **Recovery risk** is another type of credit risk that arises when lenders try to reclaim funds from a borrower who has failed to meet payment obligations. This can lead investors into long legal battles over disputes about repayment, making it difficult for them to recoup their original investments and causing additional distress in the capital markets. Investors should always thoroughly assess potential investments before entering into transactions and consider these types of risks so that they can better manage their portfolios accordingly.

Market & Liquidity Risks

Market risk refers to the potential for an investment to lose value due to factors beyond your control, such as economic conditions, political events, and natural disasters. Investors may experience large losses if they buy or sell assets at the wrong time, and this kind of risk can have a significant impact on portfolios. **Price risk** is also important as it relates to fluctuations in pricing over time, which can lead to losses due to unexpected changes in value. This kind of risk is especially pertinent for investors who hold assets for long periods since prices tend to move up and down unpredictably over extended periods of time. **Liquidity risk** refers to the difficulty of buying or selling a security without significantly affecting its price level due to lack of available buyers/ sellers at any given moment. Therefore, it is important for investors to carefully monitor their assets and stay abreast of any developments related to them so they can make informed decisions regarding their investments. Additionally, diversifying portfolios across different asset classes may help reduce the overall level of market & liquidity risks posed by individual investments.

Political Risks

Political risks are another type of capital market risk that investors should be aware of before investing. Political instability risk is the potential for a government to experience significant changes in power or policies that could significantly impact investments and their related returns. This kind of uncertainty makes it difficult for investors to predict how their portfolios may perform over time, so they must remain vigilant with regard to any news regarding political developments in order to adjust their portfolios accordingly.

Regulatory changes risk relates to the potential impacts new regulations and policies can have on investments or entire markets. Changes made by government entities such as central banks, capital market authorities or tax authorities could significantly alter how assets are treated under certain laws and regulations, which could lead to dramatic shifts in prices across all kinds of securities traded within capital markets. As such, investors should always be aware of any news related to regulatory changes so they can adjust their strategies accordingly and minimize disruption caused by unexpected developments outside of their control.

Technological Risks

Technological risks can pose a significant threat to investors in capital markets and must be taken into account when making any investment decisions. **Cybersecurity risk** is one such type of technology risk that arises from malicious actors attempting to gain unauthorized access to systems or data. This kind of risk has become increasingly common in recent years due to the growing sophistication of hacking tools and techniques, making it essential for investors to take proper measures to protect their investments from potential cyber threats. **Data security risks** are also important considerations as they relate to protecting confidential information stored on computers or other digital devices. If an investor's data is not properly secured, then malicious actors could gain access and use it for nefarious purposes, leading to financial losses or reputational damage for the affected individual or organization. As such, investors should always ensure their data is adequately protected by employing strong password protocols and regularly updating anti-virus software among other measures.

Technology-related risks also include those associated with new developments within certain industries that may have impacts on capital markets investments. For example, if a major technological breakthrough occurs in the medical field which significantly alters how treatments are administered, this could lead pharmaceutical companies' stock prices to soar while causing declines in related sectors like insurance companies which may no longer need as many policies covering these kinds of treatments anymore. Thus, understanding how technological advancements can impact different types of investments can help reduce overall exposure levels for portfolios investing across multiple asset classes in order to maximize returns while minimizing losses from market volatility caused by unexpected changes coming from outside sources.

Other Risks

Opportunity cost risk arises when investors forgo potential returns by choosing to invest in one asset over another. For example, if an investor decides to invest in stocks instead of bonds, they may miss out on higher expected returns from the bond market and suffer losses as a result. Therefore, it is important for investors to carefully assess all available options before making any investment decision so they can maximize their potential gains while minimizing losses due to opportunity costs.

Legal risks refer to issues relating specifically to legal disputes between parties involved in trading activities within capital markets. Disputes can arise due to misunderstandings about terms and conditions or failures by one party to meet its obligations under agreed-upon contracts. These kinds of disagreements can lead investors into costly court battles which can take up considerable amounts of time and resources with no guarantee that favourable outcomes will be achieved for either side. Thus, it is important for investors involved in transactions within the capital markets to ensure all relevant documentation is properly reviewed and understood prior to entering into any deal so as to minimize potential losses from legal disputes down the road.

Conclusion

It is clear that understanding and managing the various risks associated with investing in capital markets is essential for any investor seeking to maximize returns while minimizing losses. Although these risks can be daunting at times, there are strategies available to mitigate them, such as staying up-to-date on regulatory changes and ensuring all necessary documentation is properly reviewed prior to entering into a transaction. Additionally, investors should always remain aware of technological developments which may have an impact on certain asset classes so they can adjust their portfolios accordingly. By taking steps such as these, investors can protect themselves from potentially costly mistakes when participating in capital markets and ensure their investments are well-positioned for long-term success.

CHAPTER XIV

PRIMARY AND SECONDARY MARKETS

Primary and secondary markets are two distinct but interconnected parts of capital markets. The primary market is where new securities are issued, while the secondary market is where existing securities are bought and sold. Both primary and secondary markets offer a range of investments including stocks and bonds.

Primary Market

A primary market is a place where new securities are created and sold directly to investors for the first time by companies or governments through initial public offerings (IPOs) or private placements. It serves as an important source of capital for companies and governments that need to raise funds to finance their operations and projects or repay their debts.

One advantage of investing in a primary market is that it offers investors an opportunity to purchase newly issued securities at potentially lower prices than what they would find on secondary markets like exchanges since there is less competition for those assets initially compared to after they have been trading on exchanges for some time. Additionally, investors may also benefit from any price appreciation that occurs over time if those stocks perform well after being listed on exchanges or other secondary markets later down the line.

Investing in the primary market carries greater risks since there is limited information available about new companies issuing their securities; this could potentially lead to large losses if things do not go according to plan after investing in them initially during an IPO stage. Moreover, many IPOs tend to come with high costs associated with underwriting fees charged by investment banks that help facilitate their issuance, which in turn reduce returns.

Secondary Market

The secondary market is an important part of the financial system that provides liquidity and price discovery for securities issued in the primary market. The secondary market allows investors to purchase already-issued stocks, bonds, and other securities quickly and easily from other investors on exchanges or over-the-counter markets instead of directly from companies or governments issuing them. This makes it easier for investors to enter and exit positions if they need to do so during volatile periods resulting from unfavorable price movements.

Investing in secondary markets offers several advantages compared with investing in primary markets, such as greater liquidity due to more active trading; less risk since security issuers already have well-established track records; lower transaction costs associated with buying/ selling securities due to high liquidity in the market; and access to information about companies' operations.

Drivers of Price in the Secondary Market

The primary driver of price in the secondary market is supply and demand. This basic economic principle dictates that when there are more buyers than sellers, prices will rise; conversely, when there are more sellers than buyers, prices will fall. The underlying forces for these dynamics include macroeconomic factors such as interest rates or inflation which can influence investor sentiment towards different asset classes at any given time.

Other factors include events such as political disruptions, natural disasters or unfavorable news which cause uncertainty among investors leading to volatile markets where prices may be influenced by speculation rather than actual value created by fundamentals driving a specific security's performance. It is important for investors and traders to keep abreast of all news related to their investments so they can make informed decisions about how best to manage risk associated with short-term volatility while still aiming for long-term gains from profitable trades over time.

Finally, another factor impacting pricing in the secondary market is liquidity – this refers to how easily an asset can be bought or sold without significantly affecting its price level due to it being readily available amongst other potential buyers/sellers at any given moment – higher liquidity levels increase trading volume and provide greater stability compared to less liquid assets which often have wider spreads between bid & ask prices making them less attractive from an investment perspective. Ultimately understanding these drivers of demand helps create opportunities for investors looking to trade securities efficiently while maintaining good returns on their capital over time.

Risks in Primary and Secondary Markets

Price volatility risk is the potential for an asset's price to fluctuate dramatically within a short period of time due to changes in market sentiment or conditions (caused by macroeconomic factors, political instability, natural disasters or unfavorable news). Volatility creates opportunities for traders who can take advantage of rapid price movements. However, it also presents risk as any rapid changes could leave investors with significant losses if they buy or sell assets at the wrong time or they were unable to exit their positions quickly enough. This type of risk is typically higher in primary markets than that encountered when trading in secondary markets since there are fewer buyers and sellers, which can lead to more pronounced price movements.

Liquidity risk refers to how difficult it is for investors to buy or sell a security without significantly affecting its price level due to lack of available buyers/ sellers at any given moment. Most IPOs involve restricted shares which cannot be sold until certain conditions are met by investors before they can do so legally, which could lead to losses if prices drop significantly prior to meeting such conditions (because traders will not be able to access exit positions fast enough during volatile periods). In contrast, items listed on secondary exchanges usually have more established buyers/ sellers and thus offer greater liquidity as it is easier for investors needing quick access to their funds without suffering too much depreciation from market fluctuations.

Credit risk refers to the possibility that an issuer of a debt instrument may not be able to make payments on time or in full. This could potentially occur when a company goes bankrupt before its obligations have been fulfilled; such event would leave investors unable to recover their principal amount as well as any accrued interest or other benefits associated with the investment.

Overvaluation risk occurs when the value assigned to an asset by the market does not reflect the true intrinsic value created by fundamentals driving a specific security's performance. This usually happens when speculators bid stock prices up beyond what basic analysis would suggest and the result could mean that investments made during periods of high valuations could lead to large losses once reality catches up with expectations and corrects itself.

Conclusion

Investing in both primary and secondary markets offer individual investors the potential to grow their wealth over time. Investing in the primary market can lead to higher returns as newly issued assets may appreciate in value. Investments made in primary markets tend to have longer holding periods and may require more research or due diligence compared to those bought through secondary ones. Furthermore, fees associated with buying into a primary market are usually higher than those incurred when trading in a secondary one. Moreover, securities purchased from primary markets generally lack liquidity compared to those acquired via secondary markets, and investors may be unable to cash out quickly if needed or desired. Additionally, there is often less information available about companies issued on primary markets which could make it difficult for investors to properly assess an investment's value or potential return before committing resources to it. Thus, investing through either type of market should be carefully considered before being pursued actively by investors looking for long-term growth opportunities within capital markets.

CHAPTER XV

PUBLIC OFFERING

A public offering is a process in which a private company offers its shares of stock to the public for sale through a securities market. Through this offering, a company can access new capital from outside sources that are not included in its existing network of investors. This enables companies to finance large-scale projects, expand market share and pay off debts. A public offering also provides shareholders with liquidity while allowing them to diversify their investments across multiple industries and asset classes. By going through the public offering process, companies gain visibility and credibility, opening up potential collaborations and partnerships that may have been previously out of reach.

The Benefits of a Public Offering

Access to Capital

The primary benefit of a public offering is the injection of capital into the issuing company. By allowing investors to purchase shares in their business, companies are able to receive funds that can be used for growth or expansion. Additionally, being publicly listed also helps a company increase its visibility which could lead to an increased customer base and more positive brand recognition overall. Furthermore, going public gives companies access to larger pools of potential investors who may not have previously been available when operating as a private entity. Another advantage associated with a public offering is the liquidity it provides both shareholders and the issuing firm itself.

Increased Exposure

A public offering provides increased exposure to the issuing company. Going public also helps boost brand recognition which in turn can lead to an improved image and greater perceived value of the company's products and services. Such effects are especially important for smaller firms looking to increase their market share or visibility in order to compete with larger players in their respective industries. The increased exposure associated with a public offering also presents unique opportunities for firms looking to tap into international markets. Being publicly listed opens up access to global pools of capital that would otherwise be unavailable.

Attract New Investors

Going public through a public offering can be an effective way to attract new investors. By allowing members of the public to purchase part ownership in their business, companies are able to tap into larger pools of potential investors who may not have previously been available when operating as a private entity.

Create a More Liquid Market

Going public through a public offering creates a more liquid market which is beneficial for both investors and the issuing company. For shareholders, this liquidity provides them with an easier way to sell or trade their shares on secondary markets while at the same time companies can use these markets as sources for raising additional capital when needed. The increased liquidity also allows firms to better manage risk by providing them with multiple options for funding operations during periods of market volatility or uncertainty.

The added liquidity created by going public also offers significant advantages from an operational standpoint. Companies now have access to larger pools of capital which makes it easier for them to fund current projects without having to rely solely on traditional financing methods like debt instruments or venture capital. Additionally, being publicly listed helps make businesses more attractive investments since they are seen as less risky than privately held entities due to their increased transparency and ability to provide timely financial information among other features required by stock exchanges. This additional stability further enhances investor confidence which can lead to increases in share prices over time.

The Drawbacks of a Public Offering

One of the major drawbacks associated with a public offering is the cost and complexity associated with such an undertaking. Companies must engage in extensive due diligence, comply with various regulations and disclosure requirements, and incur legal fees when issuing shares to the public. Additionally, firms are also exposed to greater scrutiny from shareholders as well as regulators which can result in costly fines or penalties if certain standards are not met. Another downside of going public relates to potential conflicts between management and shareholders over issues such as executive compensation or corporate governance practices that could lead to costly litigation and other disruptions that negatively impact a firm's operations.

Compliance and Regulatory Costs Of Going Public

Compliance and regulatory costs are major considerations for any business looking to go public. Companies must ensure that all necessary paperwork is filed with the appropriate regulatory bodies in a timely manner and remain compliant with applicable laws and regulations at all times. This includes regular filings such as quarterly or annual financial statements, disclosures related to material changes in operations or ownership structure, as well as additional requirements set forth by exchanges on which the company's securities may be listed. Failure to comply with these rules can result in severe penalties or even delisting from an exchange which could significantly impact a firm's ability to raise capital or attract investors going forward. Furthermore, companies should also consider potential litigation risks associated with going public since shareholders may take action against them if they feel their interests have been harmed due to mismanagement of funds or other issues.

Underwriters' Fees

Underwriters' fees are a type of fee charged by investment banks when a company decides to go public. These fees usually include both underwriting discounts and commissions. The purpose of these fees is to cover the costs associated with researching, analyzing, marketing and selling securities in order to facilitate successful transactions for issuing companies. This includes providing guidance on pricing, selecting investors as well as helping complete paperwork and making sure all regulatory requirements are followed correctly during the entire process. As such, it's important for companies considering a public offering to understand what these costs entail before moving forward so that they can properly budget for them accordingly.

In addition to underwriter's fees there may also be other related expenses incurred throughout the public offering process such as legal or accounting services which need to be taken into account when estimating total outlays associated with going public. Furthermore, firms should keep in mind that while large public offerings often generate significant revenues due to their high valuations, small offerings may not produce enough income to fully offset these charges thus resulting in net losses overall despite having gone through this expensive procedure.

Loss of Private Company Status

Another major drawback associated with conducting a public offering is that it results in a loss of private company status. This means that once listed on an exchange, firms must comply with stringent disclosure requirements which may put them at odds with their prior policies or procedures leading to potential conflicts between shareholders and management. Furthermore, listing publicly also means increased exposure which may not be desirable for some firms looking for more privacy over their financial affairs or simply do not want greater transparency into how they are run due to competitive reasons.

Conclusion

A public offering can be a very strategic and advantageous outlet for any organization that is looking to expand and grow, and should be carefully considered before committing to such an offering. On one hand, the process allows businesses to access new sources of capital from outside their existing network of investors which can be used for financing large-scale projects, expanding market share or paying off debts. Additionally, it provides shareholders with liquidity while allowing companies to raise additional capital when needed. On the other hand, the process of going public can be a complex and costly endeavor that comes with several drawbacks, such as increased compliance and regulatory costs, underwriters' fees, and the loss of private company status. Ultimately, it is important for any company considering a public offering to weigh the advantages and drawbacks of doing so before deciding whether becoming public is right for its organization.

CHAPTER XVI

SECURITIES TRADING

Securities trading is the process of buying and selling securities such as stocks, bonds, derivatives and other securities on secondary markets (organized exchanges or over-the-counter markets). Securities trading is a way for investors to increase their capital by trading assets in order to generate returns over time. The main benefit of trading securities is that it gives people an opportunity to diversify their investments across different asset classes while also providing them with potential gains or income from dividends or interest payments. Additionally, trading securities can provide a hedge against inflation as well as help investors protect themselves from market volatility.

Market Participants in Securities Trading

Broker-dealers facilitate the buying and selling of securities. They provide advice to their clients, execute transactions on behalf of them, and charge a commission for each transaction.

Institutional investors are large financial entities such as banks, collective investment schemes, pension funds or hedge funds that invest money on behalf of their clients often in large amounts. These investors often employ sophisticated strategies such as arbitrage and leverage in order to maximize returns while minimizing risk.

Retail investors are individual investors who purchase and trade securities directly from brokerages or other financial institutions. Unlike institutional investors who typically trade large volumes of securities at once, retail traders tend to focus more on smaller transactions over shorter periods of time. This allows them to take advantage of short-term price changes rather than betting on long-term trends. Typically, retail investors buy stocks based on fundamental analysis, examining company news releases, analysts' opinions, economic reports and global events that could affect stock prices.

Securities Trading Strategies

Momentum trading is a strategy used by many investors and traders that involves buying stocks or other securities when their prices are increasing, and selling them off once they start to decline in value. Momentum traders look for companies with strong upward momentum whose price has been rapidly rising over a short period of time. They typically focus on the short-term trends rather than the long-term prospects of an asset and try to capitalize on quick profits by jumping onto the trend before it reverses course. This type of trading requires careful analysis as well as a keen understanding of market movements in order to be successful.

Value investing is another popular approach that focuses on finding undervalued assets in order to take advantage of potential market mispricing opportunities. Value investors search for securities whose current prices do not reflect their underlying worth which could eventually lead to appreciation if the stocks' true value are recognized by others in the market. The goal here is to buy low and sell high, so these investors often examine financial statements, industry trends, economic conditions, management team backgrounds and more when making decisions about what stocks to invest in.

Long-term investing is a trading strategy that involves buying stocks, bonds, or other assets and holding them for an extended period of time in order to generate returns over the long run. This approach works on the idea that stock prices tend to move up over time as companies grow and profits increase, so investors can benefit from this trend by simply buying and holding securities until they reach their desired target price or yield. Long-term investing requires patience since it often takes years before realizing any significant returns but also reduces risk since one is less exposed to market volatility which may cause short-term losses.

Day trading refers to executing transactions within one day without holding any positions overnight - meaning all trades must be completed before markets close for the day or risk incurring losses from unexpected changes during after-hours trading sessions. Day traders strive for small but consistent returns rather than large gains because this allows them to make money faster while limiting exposure to large swings that can occur between open and close each day. Day traders use technical analysis tools such as chart patterns or moving averages combined with news events and earnings reports in order to make decisions about when and what instruments should be bought/ sold during the course of one day’s session on an exchange. Day trading carries greater risk due to frequent transactions which could lead to large losses if not managed properly; however, it also offers potential rewards through increased liquidity provided by shorter holding periods compared with other strategies involving longer investment horizons.

Risk Management Strategies

Potential risks in trading securities include market risk, liquidity risk and credit risk. Market risk refers to the possibility of losses resulting from fluctuations in stock or bond prices over time. Liquidity risk is related to an investor's ability to quickly convert their assets into cash without incurring significant losses. Credit risk occurs when a borrower fails to repay a loan or other debt obligation, which could lead to the loss of principal investment amount if the lender is unable to recoup the funds owed. Other risks include financial losses due to fraud or market manipulation.

Risk management strategies involve implementing measures that help reduce exposure to potential threats while also maximizing returns on investments. These include portfolio diversification, hedging, and stop-limit orders.

Portfolio diversification is a risk management strategy that involves spreading investments across different asset classes and industries so that any sudden downturns in one area are offset by gains made elsewhere. By investing in a variety of assets, one can reap the benefits of multiple markets while limiting losses if one sector suffers an unexpected downturn. Investing in low-correlation assets helps create more stability in an investment portfolio by reducing volatility from concentrated positions.

Hedging is another widely used approach to managing risks associated with securities trading. It involves taking offsetting positions or using derivatives like options or futures contracts to protect against adverse price movements on existing holdings without liquidating them outright. Hedging reduces exposure to potential losses but it also limits upside gains since any profits earned from hedged investments are typically lower than those made through traditional equity investments due to additional transaction costs involved in executing the hedge itself.

Stop loss orders are instructions placed with brokers which automatically sell securities when they reach predetermined price levels thereby limiting an investor's potential losses on their positions. These orders provide protection should prices unexpectedly fall below expectations; however, they may not always be successful at protecting investors as there is still some degree of slippage that occurs between triggering the stop loss order and its execution resulting in unrealized losses if prices continue falling after the sale has taken place.

Securities Trading Regulations

Securities trading regulations are a set of rules and guidelines that govern the buying and selling of securities in financial markets. These regulations are designed to promote transparency, fairness, and efficiency in the trading process, and to protect investors from fraudulent or manipulative activities. Relevant regulations in securities trading include disclosure requirements for publicly traded companies such as periodic filings which provide insight into their financial performance; rules on short selling and margin trading; trading restrictions which impose restrictions on the trading of certain securities in times of market volatility or during economic crises; rules governing insider trading which prohibit using material nonpublic information for personal gain; anti-fraud provisions which aim to prevent market manipulation by spreading false information or other deceptive activities including Ponzi schemes and pump-and-dump schemes when selling securities; and customer protection requirements that ensure registered brokers are acting in clients' best interests when executing trades on their behalf.

Conclusion

Trading securities can be a rewarding way to build wealth over time but it also carries its own set of risks. Benefits include the ability to diversify portfolio, access markets with greater liquidity and potentially earn higher returns than other investments. Risks associated with securities trading include potential losses from price movements, liquidity risk, slippage when executing stop-loss orders, and financial losses due to fraud or manipulation. To minimize these risks while still taking advantage of the potential gains offered by securities markets, it is essential for investors to thoroughly research any investment decision they make and employ a suitable risk management strategy such as portfolio diversification or hedging in order to protect themselves against unexpected losses. By understanding how each security works and its underlying fundamentals before investing in it, one can reduce the chances of experiencing major losses while achieving long-term success in the secondary market.

CHAPTER XVII

DISCLOSURE REQUIREMENTS IN CAPITAL MARKETS

Capital markets are financial systems that facilitate the exchange of capital between investors and businesses. They are important for the efficient allocation of resources and for enabling economic growth. Disclosure requirements in capital markets refer to the disclosure of information by companies issuing securities to the public. This disclosure is intended to provide relevant facts about an issuing company's operations and finances to potential investors so they can make informed decisions when investing their money.

Types of Disclosure Requirements

Financial Disclosures refer to the disclosure of information related to a company's financial performance. This includes balance sheets, income statements, notes to accounts and cash flow statements which are typically required by law in order for public companies to remain compliant with relevant laws and regulations. Financial disclosures also include information regarding executive compensation, insider trading activities and related party transactions.

Disclosure of Related Party Transactions refers to the requirement for public companies to disclose any transactions conducted between them and other parties who may have an interest in their affairs, such as directors or shareholders. These disclosure requirements aim at providing transparency surrounding any potential conflicts of interests between these parties so investors can make informed decisions when investing their money.

Non-financial Disclosures involve the disclosure of information that is not directly related to a company's financial performance. This includes information about announcements regarding new products or services launched by a company, how a company plans on achieving its goals, details about research and development projects, environmental policies, and corporate social responsibility initiatives. Non-financial disclosures are voluntary disclosures- meaning they are made beyond what is legally required by a company's governing agency, and provide investors with additional insight into a company's operations or strategy which they would not otherwise have access to. Companies typically make these disclosures as part of their commitment towards providing stakeholders with greater transparency surrounding their business model and operations.

Purpose of Disclosure Requirements

The purpose of disclosure requirements in capital markets is to enhance investor information, promote market efficiency and ensure transparency. Disclosure requirements provide investors with relevant facts about a company's operations and finances so they can make informed decisions when investing their money. By providing accurate and timely information to investors, companies are able to build trust which leads to increased liquidity in the marketplace as more investors are willing to put their money into the stock market.

In addition, disclosure requirements help protect against fraud by ensuring that all parties involved in securities transactions have access to the same basic set of facts about a company or its products. Companies must also adhere to corporate governance practices, including independent directorships, audit committees and executive compensation disclosures- all intended to ensure adequate levels of transparency within public companies.

Furthermore, disclosure requirements serve an important role in helping maintain fair competition between businesses operating within capital markets. Accurate reporting on financial performance allows potential buyers or sellers of securities an equal opportunity when entering into negotiations availing both sides with access to required information needed for making investment decisions instead of relying on speculation or misinformation circulated by sources outside of official channels.

Overall, disclosure requirements play an integral role within capital markets by providing investors with relevant information necessary for making informed decisions while simultaneously protecting against fraudulent activities, promoting competition among firms, and improving overall market efficiency through greater transparency.

The Role of Regulatory Bodies in Disclosure Requirements

Regulatory bodies such as capital market authorities play a key role in ensuring that disclosure requirements are properly enforced and adhered to. These bodies establish regulations governing the disclosure practices of publicly traded companies, including the types of information they must disclose and how it should be presented. They monitor compliance with these regulations by conducting periodic inspections or reviews of company financial statements to ensure accuracy and completeness.

In addition, regulatory bodies have the authority to investigate potential violations or irregularities related to disclosures made by companies under their jurisdiction. If a violation is found, they can impose fines or other punishments depending on the severity of the breach. Furthermore, regulatory bodies often provide guidance for companies when drafting their required financial disclosures so as to minimize any potential confusion or misinterpretation from investors regarding these reports.

Finally, regulatory authorities also promote best practices among public companies when dealing with market participants such as investors and shareholders by providing guidelines on topics like corporate governance matters, executive compensation policies, and insider trading activities. This helps ensure that all parties involved in securities transactions have access to accurate information needed for making sound investment decisions.

Conclusion

Disclosure requirements in capital markets play an important role in ensuring the fairness of the marketplace and protecting investors. By providing accurate and timely information to stakeholders, companies are able to build trust which leads to increased liquidity in the stock market as more people are willing to invest their money. Furthermore, regulatory oversight of disclosure practices helps ensure that all parties involved have access to the same basic set of facts about a company and its products, thus minimizing any potential confusion or misinterpretation from investors regarding these reports. Ultimately, sound disclosure practices can help create an environment where informed decisions can be made based on real data instead of speculation or misinformation circulated by sources outside official channels.

CHAPTER XVIII

STOCK EXCHANGE LISTING RULES

Stock exchange listing rules are regulations that companies must abide by in order to be listed on a particular stock exchange. These rules outline the standards, requirements and obligations of the listed company in terms of financial information disclosure, equity standard requirements and market disclosure obligations. Adhering to these listing rules is essential for any listed company as it helps maintain trust between shareholders and investors while protecting both parties from potential risks. Furthermore, adherence to listing rules also increases transparency within the organization which can help improve investor confidence and boost returns.

Types of Stock Exchange Listing Rules

General Obligations: Generally, companies are required to comply with all applicable laws and regulations when they apply to be listed on a stock exchange. Companies must also ensure that their share structure is compliant with the listing rules of the exchange and demonstrate that their corporate governance practices meet or exceed those requirements.

Equity Standard Requirements: On top of general obligations, most exchanges have specific equity standards for listed companies. These include providing shareholders with certain information such as financial statements and reports, ensuring adequate liquidity in the company's shares, maintaining sufficient capitalization levels and regularly updating investors about relevant developments within the business.

Financial Information Requirements: Stock exchanges usually require listed companies to provide accurate financial information at regular intervals in order to maintain investor trust. This includes submitting quarterly and annual financial reports along with other documents related to transactions conducted by the company such as contracts signed in relation to mergers & acquisitions or financing activities.

Market Disclosure Requirements: In addition to general obligations and equity standard requirements, many stock exchanges require publicly traded companies to make timely market disclosures regarding any significant events occurring within their business operations such as changes in important personnel or material developments affecting performance metrics like sales figures or earnings per share (EPS). Such disclosures help protect shareholders from potential risks while allowing them access to critical information needed for informed investing decisions.

Shareholders Rights Rules

Majority Voting: Majority voting rules require companies to grant shareholders the right to vote on all matters that affect their interests. This includes electing or removing board members and approving changes in corporate governance practices such as executive compensation plans, mergers & acquisitions, and dividend policies. Having majority voting rights allows shareholders to have a say in how the company is run, which provides them with more control over their investments.

Board Structure Rules: Board structure rules stipulate how a company's board of directors should be composed and organized in order to ensure independent oversight of management decisions. These typically include requirements for balanced representation among different stakeholders such as investors and employees along with gender diversity metrics, qualifications for board membership, term limits and procedures for replacing members.

Dividend Requirements: Dividend requirements specify what type of dividends can be paid out by listed companies, when they must be distributed, who is eligible to receive them, etc. Companies are required to adhere strictly to these regulations when issuing dividends so as not to mislead or defraud investors while ensuring fairness between all classes of holding shares.

Risk Management and Compliance

Fiduciary Obligations: Fiduciary obligations involve the duties and responsibilities of a company's management to act in the best interest of its shareholders. This includes ensuring that investments are managed prudently, providing accurate financial disclosure and adhering to applicable laws and regulations.

Management Compensation Policies: Companies must establish management compensation policies that align with their overall business objectives while also taking into consideration relevant legal requirements. These policies should address issues such as executive pay scales, bonus structures, stock options and other forms of incentive-based remuneration.

Insider Trading Policies: Insider trading is prohibited by most stock exchanges as it can give certain individuals an unfair advantage over others when buying or selling securities. To prevent this from happening, companies must have clear insider trading policies in place which outline restrictions on employees' involvement in any transactions involving the company's securities along with appropriate disciplinary measures for violators.

Audit Requirements: Stock exchanges typically require listed companies to undergo an independent audit as part of their listing rules. The purpose of these audits is to verify the accuracy of financial statements provided by the company and ensure compliance with applicable accounting standards and regulations so investors can make informed decisions about investing in them without being misled or deceived by inaccurate information.

Listing Rules by Market

New York Stock Exchange Rules

The New York Stock Exchange (NYSE) is one of the oldest and largest exchanges in the world. The NYSE has a set of listing rules that companies must follow in order to be listed on the exchange. These rules cover a variety of areas, including financial requirements, corporate governance, and trading standards.

Financial requirements include minimum market capitalization, minimum shareholders' equity, and minimum earnings or revenue. Companies must also have audited financial statements and meet certain liquidity standards.

Corporate governance requirements include having an independent board of directors, an audit committee, and a code of conduct for employees.

Trading standards cover areas such as stockholder approval for certain transactions, disclosure of material information, and compliance with securities laws.

In addition to these rules, companies must also meet ongoing reporting requirements and maintain compliance with all NYSE rules and regulations. Failure to comply with these rules can result in delisting from the exchange.

London Stock Exchange Rules

The London Stock Exchange (LSE) has a set of rules and regulations that companies must follow in order to become listed on the exchange. These rules cover various areas such as eligibility criteria, disclosure requirements, shareholder rights, and ongoing obligations.

To be eligible for listing, a company must meet certain financial and governance criteria, including having a minimum market capitalization and a track record of profitability. The company must also provide detailed information about its business, financial performance, and ownership structure, and appoint a sponsor to oversee the listing process.

Once listed, companies must comply with ongoing disclosure requirements, such as providing regular financial reports and making timely announcements about any material developments. Shareholders are also granted certain rights, such as the ability to vote on important matters and receive dividends.

The London Stock Exchange also enforces rules aimed at maintaining the integrity and transparency of the market, including rules governing insider trading and market abuse. Companies that fail to comply with the rules may face sanctions, including delisting from the exchange.

Nasdaq Rules

Nasdaq is one of the most prominent stock markets around the world with many high-profile tech companies being listed on it. The Nasdaq Stock Market has a set of listing requirements that companies must meet in order to be listed on the exchange. These rules are designed to ensure that companies are financially stable and transparent, and that they meet certain governance standards. The rules cover a wide range of areas, including financial requirements, such as minimum stockholders' equity and market capitalization; corporate governance requirements, such as the composition of the board of directors and the independence of audit committees; and disclosure requirements, such as timely and accurate reporting of financial results and other material events. Companies that fail to comply with these rules may be subject to delisting from the Nasdaq Stock Market.

Hong Kong Stock Exchange Rules

Hong Kong has established itself as a premier destination for international listings thanks to its relatively simple yet stringent listing rules designed not only to attract more foreign investments but also to ensure investor protection at all times. The Hong Kong Stock Exchange has a set of listing rules which govern the eligibility requirements for companies seeking to list on the exchange. The rules require that companies have a minimum track record of operations and profitability, as well as a minimum market capitalization. The rules also set out requirements for the disclosure of financial information, corporate governance, and shareholder rights. Companies must appoint a sponsor to assist with the listing process and ensure compliance with the rules.

Once listed, companies must continue to comply with ongoing disclosure and reporting requirements, as well as maintain a minimum level of public float.

Conclusion

Stock exchange listing rules are important for investor protection and a successful capital market. Without these regulations in place, companies would be free to commit fraudulent activities such as insider trading or providing misleading financial statements which could severely damage trust in the market. In order to ensure compliance with these standards and protect investors' interests, listed companies must abide by the requirements of their respective exchanges including providing accurate financial information at regular intervals, making timely disclosures about material developments within their business operations, granting majority voting rights to shareholders, and establishing appropriate management compensation policies. By adhering to these strict listing criteria, companies can build greater investor confidence and also gain access to new sources of capital.

CHAPTER XIX

MEASURING THE PERFORMANCE OF STOCK MARKETS

Stock markets are financial centers where securities are bought and sold. They provide a platform for companies to issue stocks, bonds, and other securities. This allows investors to gain access to a wide range of investments with the potential for returns that far exceed those available in traditional savings accounts or money market funds. Stock markets also allow companies to raise capital through public offerings, which helps fuel economic growth by providing additional capital for businesses to expand their operations. By connecting buyers and sellers together on an organized exchange, stock markets facilitate efficient price discovery while ensuring liquidity in the market. Furthermore, they offer investors an opportunity to diversify their portfolios by offering exposure to different types of investments.

Measuring the performance of stock markets is essential for investors to make informed decisions. Several methods are employed in order to assess the success of a particular market, such as analyzing changes in share prices, monitoring trading volume, studying the number of listed companies on an exchange, and evaluating economic indicators. **Share prices** offer insight into how well a company's stocks have been performing over time; this can be done by tracking both short-term and long-term trends. **Trading volume** provides information about how much activity is occurring in a given stock market; higher volumes indicate more liquidity while lower levels may suggest stagnation or decline. The **total number of listed companies** gives valuable information regarding the breadth of investments available within an exchange; greater numbers imply that there are more opportunities available for investment diversification. Lastly, it is beneficial to consider **economic indicators** such as unemployment rates, inflation levels and GDP growth when assessing stock market performance since these factors often impact investor sentiment which can drive price fluctuations in either direction.

Why Stock Market Success Matters

Assessing the performance of stock markets is an essential part of financial management. By evaluating how a particular market is doing, investors can gain valuable insight into whether or not their investments are likely to yield positive returns in the future. Additionally, assessing stock market performance allows for informed decision-making when it comes to diversifying portfolios and allocating funds appropriately. This helps ensure that investors have access to a broad range of investment opportunities while mitigating risk through smart portfolio design.

Stock market success also matters from both an economic and political perspective. As stock prices rise, companies become more profitable which leads to increased job creation and higher wages for workers; this has a direct impact on economic growth as well as consumer spending habits which further stimulates the economy as a whole. Furthermore, strong stock markets often serve as indicators of overall confidence in governments and their respective policies; if citizens trust that government decisions will lead towards greater prosperity then they may be more likely to invest in company stocks which then boosts investor sentiment even further thus creating a virtuous cycle of growth and development.

Conclusion

Measuring stock market success is of paramount importance for investors, businesses and governments alike. By analyzing share prices, trading volumes and the number of listed companies on an exchange, investors can gain valuable insight into how well stocks are performing over time as well as what opportunities exist for diversifying portfolios and mitigating risk. Furthermore, economic indicators such as inflation levels and GDP growth should also be taken into consideration when assessing stock market performance since these factors have a direct impact on investor sentiment which in turn influences price fluctuations. Ultimately, measuring stock market success helps ensure that decisions regarding investments are made with full knowledge of current conditions; this ultimately leads to more informed decision-making and increased chances of financial success in the long run.

CHAPTER XX

MAJOR STOCK EXCHANGES GLOBALLY

Stock markets play a crucial role in the global economy, enabling companies to raise capital, investors to build wealth, and economies to grow. While there are numerous stock exchanges around the world, a few major ones stand out due to their size, liquidity, and influence on global financial markets.

New York Stock Exchange (NYSE) - United States

Established in 1792, the New York Stock Exchange is the largest and most influential stock market in the world. Located in New York City's financial district, the NYSE is home to many of the world's largest and most well-known companies. The NYSE serves as a marketplace for buying and selling stocks, bonds, and other financial instruments. As of March 2023, the NYSE had a market capitalization of over 25 trillion USD*, making it a significant driver of global financial markets.

The NYSE operates under an auction model, where buyers and sellers come together to determine the prices of securities through supply and demand. It uses a system of designated market makers (DMMs) who act as intermediaries to facilitate trading and maintain market liquidity. The exchange also employs state-of-the-art technology to ensure fast, secure, and efficient trading.

NASDAQ - United States

Launched in 1971, the NASDAQ (National Association of Securities Dealers Automated Quotations) is the second-largest stock exchange in the world by market capitalization. As of March 2023, the NASDAQ had a market capitalization of about 19 trillion USD*.

Known for its electronic trading platform, the NASDAQ is home to many technology and internet-based companies, including giants like Apple, Amazon, Google parent company

Alphabet, and Facebook. It is also the preferred exchange for many smaller, high-growth companies and startups in various industries. As of 2021, there were more than 3,000 companies listed on the Nasdaq Stock Market. The Nasdaq Composite Index is a popular benchmark for U.S. technology stocks, reflecting the performance of the technology sector and the broader market.

Shanghai Stock Exchange (SSE) - China

Founded in 1990, the Shanghai Stock Exchange is the largest stock market in China and the third-largest globally by market capitalization. As of March 2023, the SSE had a market capitalization of over 7.2 trillion USD*. The SSE is headquartered in Shanghai, China's financial hub, and primarily trades in stocks, bonds, and funds. The SSE is home to many large state-owned Chinese enterprises, as well as prominent private companies like Alibaba and Tencent.

The SSE has two main trading boards: the Main Board, and the Science and Technology Innovation Board (STAR Market). The Main Board is comprised of the SSE Composite Index (SSECI), which lists all stocks traded on the exchange, and the SSE 50 and SSE 180 indices, which consist of the largest and most representative companies listed on the exchange. The STAR Market, launched in 2019, is designed to support innovative and high-tech companies, particularly those in emerging industries such as biotechnology, information technology, and advanced manufacturing. The listing and trading requirements for the STAR Market are more relaxed than those of the Main Board, allowing start-ups and growth-oriented companies to access public financing more easily.

Euronext - Europe

Formed in 2000 through the merger of the Amsterdam, Brussels, and Paris stock exchanges, Euronext is the largest stock exchange in Europe. Since then, it has expanded its scope to include additional exchanges, such as the Irish Stock Exchange and the Oslo Stock Exchange, and now operates markets in several European countries, including Belgium, France, Ireland, the Netherlands, Norway, and Portugal. The exchange is home to many notable European companies, such as L'Oréal, Airbus, and Royal Dutch Shell. As of March 2023, Euronext had a market capitalization of over 6.7 trillion USD*.

Tokyo Stock Exchange (TSE) - Japan

Established in 1878, the Tokyo Stock Exchange (TSE) is home to Japan's most significant companies, including automotive giants Toyota and Honda, as well as global electronics companies like Sony and Panasonic.

The TSE is organized into several market sections, including the First Section, Second Section, Mothers (Market of the high-growth and emerging stocks), and JASDAQ (for small and medium-sized enterprises). The exchange lists various types of securities, including stocks, bonds, ETFs, REITs, and derivatives. As of March 2023, the TSE had a market capitalization of 5.6 trillion USD*. The exchange currently uses the "arrowhead" trading system, which enables high-speed and low-latency trading for market participants.

Major African Exchanges

African exchanges play a significant role in the economic development of the continent, providing a platform for companies to raise capital and investors to diversify their portfolios. Major African Stock Exchanges include the Johannesburg Stock Exchange, the Nigerian Stock Exchange, the Casablanca Stock Exchange, the Egyptian Stock Exchange and the Nairobi Securities Exchange.

Johannesburg Stock Exchange (JSE) - South Africa

Established in 1887, the JSE is the largest and oldest stock exchange in Africa with a market capitalization of over 1.3 trillion USD**. The JSE operates under a fully electronic trading system, which allows for efficient and transparent transactions. It is home to a diverse range of companies across various sectors, including mining, financial services, retail, and telecommunications. Notable listings include Naspers, Anglo American, and Sasol.

The JSE is also known for its market indices, such as the FTSE/JSE Africa All Share Index, which tracks the performance of the largest companies listed on the exchange. The JSE also offers other financial products and services, such as bonds, derivatives, and exchange-traded funds (ETFs), catering to the diverse needs of investors.

Nigerian Stock Exchange (NSE) - Nigeria

Founded in 1960, the Nigerian Stock Exchange (NSE) is the second-largest exchange in Africa with a market capitalization of over 66 billion USD**. Notable listings include Dangote Cement, MTN Nigeria, and Nigerian Breweries. It provides a platform for various financial instruments, including equities, bonds, and exchange-traded funds (ETFs) to be traded by investors.

The Nigerian Stock Exchange is divided into several market segments, including the Main Board, the Premium Board, and the Alternative Securities Market (ASeM). The Main Board primarily caters to established companies with proven track record, while the Premium Board targets companies that adhere to the highest corporate governance standards. The ASeM focuses on small and medium-sized enterprises (SMEs) with potential for growth. The NSE operates an electronic trading platform, which has enhanced the efficiency, transparency, and accessibility of the market.

Casablanca Stock Exchange (CSE) - Morocco

Founded in 1929, the Casablanca Stock Exchange (CSE) is the third-largest exchange in Africa with a market capitalization of over 65 billion USD**. Notable listings include Maroc Telecom, Attijariwafa Bank, and BCP. Located in the city of Casablanca, the exchange plays a vital role in the Moroccan economy by facilitating the trading of shares, bonds, and other financial instruments.

The Casablanca Stock Exchange has two main market segments: the Main Market and the Development Market. The Main Market is for well-established companies with a proven track record, while the Development Market caters to small and medium-sized enterprises (SMEs) that show significant growth potential.

Egyptian Exchange (EGX) - Egypt

Established in 1883, The Egyptian Exchange (EGX), formerly known as the Cairo and Alexandria Stock Exchange, is one of the oldest stock exchanges in the Middle East and Africa with a market capitalization of over 35 billion USD**. Notable listings include Telecom Egypt, Commercial International Bank, and Orascom Construction.

The EGX consists of two main markets: the Main Market and the Nile Stock Exchange (NILEX) for small and medium-sized enterprises. The Main Market comprises the largest and most established companies in Egypt, while the Nile Stock Exchange focuses on providing a platform for small and medium-sized enterprises (SMEs) to raise capital and promote growth. The EGX offers various types of securities, including stocks, bonds, and exchange-traded funds (ETFs), catering to a diverse range of investors.

Some of the key indices tracked on the Egyptian Exchange include the EGX 30 Index, which consists of the top 30 companies by market capitalization, the EGX 50 EWI Index, representing the top 50 equally weighted companies, and the EGX 70 EWI Index, focusing on the next 70 equally weighted companies after the top 50.

Nairobi Securities Exchange (NSE) - Kenya

Established in 1954, the Nairobi Securities Exchange (NSE) is the leading securities exchange in East Africa with a market capitalization of over 17 billion USD**. Notable listings include Safaricom, Equity Group Holdings, and East African Breweries. The NSE offers various financial products and services, including equities, bonds, and derivatives.

Conclusion

These major stock markets play a critical role in shaping the global economic landscape and fostering economic growth and development. They provide a platform for companies to raise capital, investors to generate returns, and governments to regulate and oversee financial markets. As global economies continue to evolve, these stock exchanges will remain influential in guiding the direction of financial markets and fostering economic growth on a global scale.

* Source: https://www.statista.com/

** Source: https://sashares.co.za/

CHAPTER XXI

MAJOR STOCK MARKET CRASHES

Investing in the stock market can be an exciting and profitable venture. However, with great reward comes great risk. Throughout history, there have been several instances where the stock market crashed, causing widespread panic and financial devastation. Below are some of the most significant stock market crashes that have occurred around the world.

The Wall Street Crash of 1929

The Wall Street Crash of 1929 was one of the most significant events in modern economic history. It marked the end of the Roaring Twenties, a period of unprecedented economic growth and prosperity in the United States, and the beginning of the Great Depression, a decade-long period of economic hardship and social upheaval.

The causes of the Wall Street Crash are complex and multifaceted, but at its core, the crash was the result of a speculative bubble in the stock market. In the years leading up to the crash, investors had poured billions of dollars into the stock market, driving up prices and creating a sense of euphoria and optimism. But this optimism was based on little more than blind faith and speculation, and when the bubble burst, the consequences were catastrophic.

The crash was caused by a number of factors, including over-speculation in the stock market, which led to inflated prices; a decline in consumer spending, which led to a decrease in demand for goods and services; a rise in interest rates, which made it more expensive for businesses to borrow money; and a decline in agricultural prices, which hurt farmers and led to a decrease in demand for manufactured goods.

On October 24, 1929, known as **Black Thursday**, the stock market experienced a sudden and dramatic decline in value, triggering a panic among investors. Over the next several days, the market continued to plummet, wiping out billions of dollars in wealth and leaving millions of investors destitute.

The stock market lost over 30 billion USD in value, which is equivalent to over 400 billion USD today. Millions of people lost their jobs, homes, and savings. The Great Depression also led to a decline in international trade and a rise in nationalism. The crash also led to a number of reforms in the financial industry, including the creation of the Securities and Exchange Commission (SEC).

The Black Monday Crash of 1987

October 19, 1987, also known as **Black Monday**, is the day the US stock market experienced its largest one-day percentage drop in history. The Dow Jones Industrial Average plummeted 22%, erasing 500 billion USD in market value. To put that into perspective, that is equivalent to 1.2 trillion USD in today's dollars. The crash was so severe that it took two years for the market to fully recover. The crash also caused significant declines in stock markets around the world.

There are a number of factors that contributed to the Black Monday crash. One factor was the use of portfolio insurance, a trading strategy that involves selling stocks when prices fall. This strategy can lead to a self-fulfilling prophecy, as selling can cause prices to fall even further. Another factor that contributed to the crash was the use of computer-driven trading. Computers can trade very quickly, and this can lead to a rapid sell-off if prices start to fall. Other contributing factors include rising interest rates, falling oil prices, and a weakening US dollar.

The Black Monday crash had a significant impact on the global economy. It led to a decline in stock prices, a decrease in investment, and a rise in unemployment.

The Japanese Asset Price Bubble Burst of 1990

The Japanese asset price bubble of the late 1980s was at its peak in 1990. The value of land and stocks in Japan was estimated to be worth over 4 times the entire US GDP. Japan was caught up in a frenzy of speculation and excess. As the economy boomed in the 1980s, investors poured money into real estate and stocks, driving up prices. At its peak, the price of land in Tokyo was estimated to be worth more than all of the land in the United States. The Japanese asset price bubble was the result of a combination of factors, including deregulation, low-interest rates, and speculation.

The bubble was characterized by a rapid acceleration of asset prices and overheated economic activity, as well as an uncontrolled money supply and credit expansion. More specifically, over-confidence and speculation regarding asset and stock prices were closely associated with excessive monetary easing policy at the time.

In 1990, the Bank of Japan raised interest rates in an attempt to cool down the overheating economy. This had the unintended effect of bursting the asset price bubble. As prices plummeted, investors who had borrowed heavily to invest in real estate and stocks found themselves underwater, unable to repay their loans.

The fallout was devastating. Banks and other financial institutions that had lent heavily to speculators found themselves with large amounts of bad debt on their books. Many people lost their jobs and their life savings. The burst of the bubble also had an impact on the country's culture, as people had to adjust to a new way of life that was characterized by economic hardship. The bursting of the asset price bubble had a number of negative consequences, including a decline in investment and economic growth, a rise in unemployment and bankruptcies, a decline in consumer spending, and a decline in the value of the Japanese yen.

The Japanese government attempted to prop up these institutions with massive bailouts, but the damage had already been done. The Japanese economy would spend the next two decades mired in stagnation and deflation. The effects of the bubble burst were felt not only in Japan but also around the world, as the country's economy was closely tied to the global economy.

The Asian Financial Crisis of 1997

The Asian Financial Crisis originated in Thailand, where the government had been borrowing heavily to fund infrastructure projects. The country's currency, the baht, became overvalued, and investors began to pull out. This sparked a domino effect, causing financial problems in neighbouring countries like Indonesia, South Korea, and Malaysia.

The crisis had significant macroeconomic-level effects, including sharp reductions in the values of currencies, stock markets, and other asset prices of several Asian countries. The nominal U.S. dollar GDP of ASEAN fell by 9 billion USD in 1997 and 218 billion USD in 1998. In South Korea, the 170 billion USD fall in 1998 was equal to 33% of the 1997 GDP. Many businesses collapsed, and as a consequence, millions of people fell below the poverty line in 1997–1998. Indonesia, South Korea, and Thailand were the countries most affected by the crisis.

There were a number of factors that contributed to the Asian financial crisis, including:

- Over-borrowing by corporations and banks. Many corporations and banks in Asia had borrowed heavily in foreign currencies, particularly US dollars. This made them vulnerable to changes in the value of their currencies.
- Speculation in the stock market. There was a lot of speculation in the stock markets of Asia in the years leading up to the crisis. This led to inflated stock prices, which were then vulnerable to a crash.

- Loss of confidence in the financial system. When the crisis began, there was a loss of confidence in the financial systems of Asia. This led to a decline in lending and investment, which further exacerbated the crisis.

The Asian financial crisis had a significant impact on the economies of Asia. It led to a decline in economic growth, an increase in unemployment, and a decline in living standards. The crisis also had a negative impact on the global economy. It led to a decline in trade and investment, and it contributed to the slowdown in economic growth of the United States and Europe.

The Dot-Com Bubble Burst of 2000

The dot-com bubble was a period of rapid economic growth and inflated stock prices in the United States, primarily driven by the rise of internet-based companies. The bubble began in the late 1990s and peaked in March 2000, when the Nasdaq Composite index reached a high of 5,048. The bubble burst soon after, and the Nasdaq lost over 75% of its value by October 2002.

Companies that had been valued in the billions of dollars just a few months earlier were suddenly worth next to nothing. Investors lost their money, and employees of these companies found themselves out of a job. Many of these dot-com companies were based on nothing more than an idea and a flashy website. They had no real business plan, no revenue stream, and no way of making money in the long term. But investors were so caught up in the hype that they didn't bother to look at the fundamentals. There were a number of factors that contributed to the dot-com bubble, including:

- Low-interest rates. The Federal Reserve kept interest rates low in the late 1990s, which made it easier for people to borrow money and invest in stocks.
- Easy access to capital. Venture capitalists and other investors were eager to invest in internet-based companies, even those with no track record of profitability.
- Exaggerated expectations. Many investors were convinced that the Internet would revolutionize the economy and that internet-based companies would become the next big thing.

The dot-com bubble burst when investors began to realize that many of the internet-based companies were not profitable and that their stock prices were based on unrealistic expectations. This led to a wave of selling, which caused the stock market to crash.

The dot-com bubble burst had a significant impact on the U.S. economy. It led to a decline in economic growth, an increase in unemployment, and a decline in living standards. It also had a negative impact on the global economy. It led to a decline in trade and investment, and it contributed to the slowdown in economic growth of other countries.

The Global Financial Crisis of 2008

The Global Financial Crisis of 2008 was a severe worldwide economic crisis that developed in 2007 and became more severe in 2008. It was the most serious financial crisis since the Great Depression of the 1930s.

The crisis was caused by a number of factors, including subprime lending and the housing bubble. **Subprime lending** is the practice of lending money to borrowers with poor credit histories. This type of lending became widespread in the United States in the early 2000s. The **housing bubble** was a period of rapid increase in housing prices in the United States. This bubble was fueled by subprime lending and easy access to credit.

People were buying homes left and right, even if they couldn't afford them. Banks were more than happy to lend them the money because they could make a quick profit by selling those mortgages to investors. These investors then bundled those mortgages into securities that were sold to other investors.

The housing bubble burst in 2007, which led to a decline in housing prices and a wave of foreclosures. People couldn't afford their mortgages, and they started defaulting in droves. Investors realized that those securities they had bought were now worthless. Banks started going under, and the economy started to spiral out of control.

Banks were also lending money to each other during the housing bubble through the interbank market to meet their reserve requirements. When the housing market crashed, banks started getting nervous. They didn't know who was holding all those worthless securities, and they didn't want to lend money to each other anymore. The interbank market froze up, and banks started going under.

When the economy started to spiral out of control, the government stepped in and passed the Troubled Asset Relief Program (TARP), which gave banks billions of dollars to try to stabilize their operations. They also passed the American Recovery and Reinvestment Act (ARRA), which injected money into the economy to try to jump-start it again.

The Financial Crisis of 2008 had a significant impact on the global economy. It led to a decline in economic growth, an increase in unemployment, and a decline in living standards. The crisis also had a negative impact on the global financial system. It led to a decline in lending and investment, and it contributed to the slowdown in economic growth of other countries.

The Flash Crash of 2010

The 2010 Flash Crash was a major stock market crash that occurred on May 6, 2010. It was the largest one-day percentage decline in stock market history since Black Monday. The Dow Jones Industrial Average (DJIA) lost over 9% of its value in just minutes, before recovering most of its losses by the end of the day. The crash was caused by a number of factors, including:

- A sell-off in the stock market. The stock market had been on a downward trend in the weeks leading up to the crash. This trend was exacerbated by concerns about the European debt crisis and the global economic slowdown.
- A large sell order. A large sell order for S&P 500 futures contracts was placed, which triggered a wave of selling that led to a sharp decline in stock prices.
- The use of high-frequency trading. High-frequency trading is a type of trading that uses computers to buy and sell stocks very quickly. This type of trading can amplify market volatility, as it can lead to large orders being placed very quickly.

The Flash Crash had a significant impact on the stock market and the global economy. It led to a decline in investor confidence and a slowdown in economic growth. The crash also led to calls for regulation of high-frequency trading.

The China Stock Market Crash of 2015

The 2015 China stock market crash was a period of sharp decline in the Chinese stock market that began in June 2015 and ended in early February 2016. The China Shanghai Composite Index lost nearly 40% of its value in just a few months.

The crash was triggered by a combination of factors, including a slowdown in China's economic growth, a decrease in exports, concerns about the country's currency, over-speculation, and loss of confidence in the financial system. Investors who had poured money into Chinese stocks were left with huge losses, and many were forced to sell off their assets to cover their losses.

The Chinese government intervened in the stock market in an attempt to stop the crash. This intervention included buying stocks, lowering interest rates, and providing liquidity to the market.

The China stock market crash had a significant impact on the Chinese economy. It led to a decline in economic growth, an increase in unemployment, and a decline in living standards. The crash also had a negative impact on the global economy. It led to a decline in trade and investment, and it contributed to the slowdown in economic growth of other countries.

The COVID-19 Market Crash

The COVID-19 pandemic took a toll on the global economy, and the stock market had not been spared. The COVID-19 Crash of 2020 was a period of sharp decline in stock markets around the world that began in February 2020 and ended in April 2020. Investors saw their portfolios shrink as the stock market crashed. The pandemic caused widespread panic and uncertainty, leading to a decline in consumer spending. This directly affected the stock market, with many companies experiencing a decrease in sales and revenue. As a result, stock prices fell, and investors suffered losses. The crash was caused by a number of factors, including:

- The COVID-19 pandemic. The COVID-19 pandemic was a global health crisis that led to widespread economic disruption. The pandemic caused businesses to close, people to lose their jobs, and consumers to cut back on spending. This led to a decline in demand for goods and services, which in turn led to a decline in economic growth.
- Fear and uncertainty. The COVID-19 pandemic caused a great deal of fear and uncertainty among investors. This led to a decline in investor confidence, which made investors more likely to sell stocks.

The COVID-19 Crash of 2020 had a significant impact on the global economy. It led to a decline in economic growth, an increase in unemployment, and a decline in living standards. The crash also had a negative impact on the global financial system. It led to a decline in lending and investment, and it contributed to the slowdown in economic growth of other countries.

Conclusion

These are just a few examples of the major stock market crashes that have occurred throughout history. While they can be devastating, they also serve as a reminder of the risks associated with investing in the stock market.

www.ingramcontent.com/pod-product-compliance
Lightning Source LLC
LaVergne TN
LVHW061253100826
845148LV00008B/1112

* 9 7 8 1 7 3 4 3 5 3 7 5 4 *